Advertising Media Sourcebook

FOURTH EDITION

YO-DCH-288

Advertising
Media
Sourcebook
FOURTH EDITION

Peter B. Turk
Donald W. Jugenheimer
Arnold M. Barban

Printed on recyclable paper

NTC Business Books
a division of *NTC Publishing Group* • Lincolnwood, Illinois USA

Library of Congress Cataloging-in-Publication Data

Turk, Peter B.
 Advertising media sourcebook / Peter B. Turk, Donald W.
Jugenheimer, Arnold M. Barban. -- 4th ed.
  p.   cm.
 Barban's name appears first on the earlier edition.
 Includes index.
 ISBN 0-8442-3521-0 (alk. paper)
 1. Advertising media planning--United States. I. Jugenheimer,
Donald W. II. Barban, Arnold M. III. Title.
HF5826.5.A38 1996
659.1'0973--dc20   96-20269
                                                         CIP

Published by NTC Business Books, a division of NTC Publishing Group.
© 1997 by NTC Publishing Group, 4255 West Touhy Avenue,
Lincolnwood (Chicago), Illinois 60646–1975 U.S.A.
Manufactured in the United States of America.

6 7 8 9 ML 0 9 8 7 6 5 4 3 2 1

Contents

Acknowledgments

The source examples are reproduced through the courtesy of the following firms and organizations:

Arbitron Ratings Company

Audit Bureau of Circulations

Editor & Publisher Market Guide

Leading National Advertisers, Inc.

Mediamark Research, Inc.

Nielsen Media Research Company

Radio Advertising Bureau

Sales & Marketing Management

Simmons Market Research Bureau: *Study of Media and Markets*

Standard Rate and Data Service

VNU Media Watch

The authors express their appreciation to Professor Lee F. Young of the University of Kansas, who contributed significantly as a coauthor of the first two editions of this book.

I·N·T·R·O·D·U·C·T·I·O·N

Planning and Buying Advertising Media

The process by which media positions are selected by companies or their agencies is a complex one involving substantial marketing and advertising research. While the process includes numerous steps, it operates in two stages: media planning and media buying. Because this book demonstrates sources of information for both stages, it is important to outline major elements in each stage.

Media Planning

Planning is the strategic formulation of activities designed to carry out the goals or objectives of the advertising program. The planner's decisions are directed by a series of questions:

1. Whom is the campaign directed to? Answering this question means identifying the target audiences of greatest value to the marketer. Planners work with audience descriptions based on demographic measurements, lifestyle data, behavioral measures such as sales experience, and others in usage and loyalty. The planner must match these research profiles with media profiles to recommend target media opportunities.

2. Where will the campaign run? Any company with more than one outlet for sale has to make geographic decisions for advertising programs. The decisions concern several directions including: the number of markets, the boundaries of the markets selected, and allocation of dollars between markets. These marketing decisions heavily influence the media considered by planners even for firms that distribute products or services nationally.

3. How long will the campaign run? While most consumer marketers offer products and services year-round, few advertising budgets can sustain continuous efforts. Planning must reflect continuity strategy that balances factors such as the carryover effect of promotions, competitors' activities, and consumer usage patterns.

4. When will the campaign run? Time decisions are not limited to the length of the advertising program. Planners must also deal with desired emphasis on months, weeks, days, and even parts of the day. Included in this consideration are product life cycles, seasonal usage levels, and media popularity (availability of target audiences) and scheduling flexibility.

5. What degree of target coverage and repetition of exposure are necessary? The terms *reach* and *frequency* are fundamental to the success of any advertising plan. *Reach* concerns the extent of target audience coverage (how many different prospects will have message exposure opportunity). *Frequency* estimates repeated exposures within a given timeline. Target audiences for many firms are elusive, and planners must compromise or balance levels of reach or frequency. Sound media research is essential to accurate estimation.

1

In summary, media planning demands a strong marketing data foundation along with a solid understanding of advertising media dynamics. Dependable research measurements are vital in answering these campaign plan questions.

Media Buying

If media planners are the architects of advertising plans, then media buyers are the construction companies or builders. Plans are only ideas until they are tactically completed. Someone must choose the television program, radio station, newspaper, or outdoor location. Buyers are the specialists with responsibility for the actual advertising schedules that complete the media process. Here are some of the major functions of media buying.

1. Vehicle selection.   The placement of the advertising message involves choosing each communication channel location. Location decisions are based on quantitative information on audience size and composition, and on qualitative factors such as selling atmosphere and product harmony. Because vehicles must be selected in advance of the campaign, estimations must be made as forecasts. Media research sources are critical in vehicle assessments.

2. Contract negotiation.   With many vehicle alternatives, and many potential advertisers, it is not surprising that most media buys are negotiated transactions. The seller wants a high advertiser dollar, and buyers seek maximum value for minimum cost. Buyers negotiate for price, for message position, for guaranteed audience levels, or for promotional extras as contract collateral. It is a skillful competition with expert adversaries.

3. Meet planning goals.   Media plans utilize quantitative criteria to satisfy program objectives. Reach and frequency levels, rating points, and cost-per-thousand are set in absolute figures. The buying function is expected to build schedules capable of meeting these requirements. All levels must be accommodated within budgetary constraints.

4. Monitor performance.   As explained, media schedules must often be contracted for well in advance of the starting date. Public consumption of media is not a stable activity. Things change. Buyers must review all available media research to assure that expected performance of the selected vehicles is attained. For those media with frequent research measurement, monitoring can be a weekly duty.

5. Schedule maintenance.   What happens if TV programs are preempted, if print materials don't arrive in time for printing, or if weather stops the radio station's transmission? Schedules have to be shifted, vehicles have to be replaced and substituted for. The buying function does not stop until the campaign is over and all affidavits and bills are accounted for.

Success of media plans is fully dependent upon the skillful creation of advertising media schedules by buying departments. Similarly, reliable sources of data and information are essential in the execution of the campaign.

Staging the Advertising Media Process

To better demonstrate how media planning and buying fit in marketing communication, a flow diagram is shown in Figure 1. Here are some brief observations to assist your understanding of the model's function.

1. Source diversity.   Notice the variety of research inputs needed to make the model operational. Marketing research prepares the *"Objective"* section. Media research plays several important roles in *"Planning"* and *"Implementation."* Advertising campaign effectiveness research is crucial in impact *"Evaluation."*

2. Closed-end model.   To make full use of a campaign investment, the media planning and buying contributions to effectiveness must be evaluated. The results are then given natural access to plans for the next campaign cycle. This insures that media is a complete function in advertising decision-making.

3. Competitive awareness.   Throughout the process, data and information of competing strategies and tactics is needed. Consumer marketing companies, though driven by consumer satisfaction, must compete with others for target prospect attention and interest. Media plans must reflect knowledge of what competitors are doing.

FIGURE 1.
OVERVIEW OF THE DECISION-MAKING PROCESS

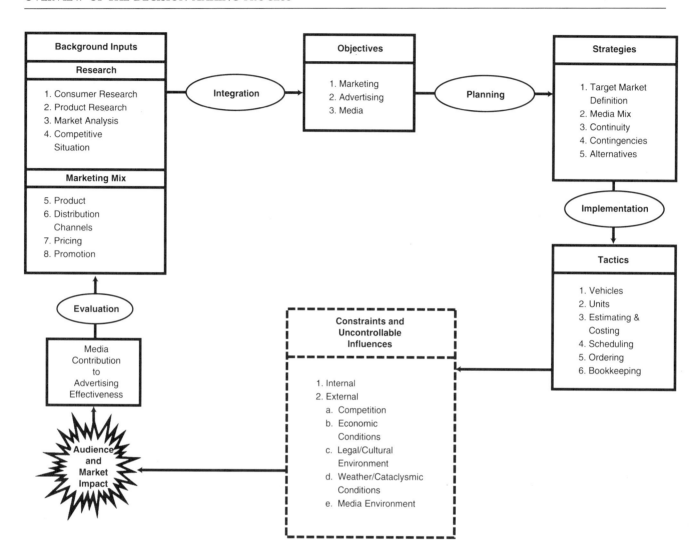

Checklist Steps for the Media Decision Process

To expand Figure 1, the following outline suggests a number of operations that may be used to fulfill each stage in the model operation. The checklist shown is intended to be optimal. Each marketing organization would tailor the list to its own specifications.

Research Inputs
- ☐ Analyze the product or service to be advertised.
- ☐ Analyze the market.
  - ☐ Determine market potential.
- ☐ Perform consumer research.
- ☐ Gather background information on the activities of the competition.

Goals
- ☐ Establish the marketing objectives.
  - ☐ Establish specific level of accomplishment that is desired against which eventual success is measured.
  - ☐ Determine plans for product development.
    - ☐ Utilize the marketing concept.
  - ☐ Outline introduction patterns (for new or altered products).
  - ☐ Establish pricing policy.
  - ☐ Develop general patterns of timing (by year, season, month, week, and/or day of week).
  - ☐ Determine distribution availabilities and geographic patterns.
  - ☐ Initiate plans for dealing with competition.
  - ☐ Examine need for service operations.
  - ☐ Outline goals of promotional activities.
  - ☐ Plan promotional support.
- ☐ Establish the advertising objectives.
  - ☐ Support marketing objectives.
  - ☐ Establish levels to achieve in awareness, knowledge, desire for product, and sales.
  - ☐ Introduce general media characteristics that are to be considered.
  - ☐ Outline basic creative considerations.
  - ☐ Determine budget levels.
  - ☐ Consider other promotional efforts that will support advertising.
    - ☐ Allocate budget to various functions, goals, products, and so forth.
  - ☐ Specify timing patterns of advertising.
- ☐ Establish the media objectives.
  - ☐ Support marketing and advertising objectives.
  - ☐ Outline basic audience characteristics to be considered.
  - ☐ Establish need for reach, frequency, continuity, and impact.
    - ☐ Determine the relative importance of reach, frequency, continuity, and impact.
    - ☐ Attempt to establish specific levels of reach, frequency, continuity, and impact that are to be achieved.
    - ☐ Consider media "wave" patterns.
  - ☐ Establish cost efficiency goals and criteria for advertising media to be selected.
  - ☐ Examine need for flexibility in advertising media.

Strategies
- ☐ Evaluate proposed advertising budget.
  - ☐ Relate budget investment to sales expectations.
  - ☐ Justify budgetary changes and trends.

☐ Determine the target group.
    ☐ Outline specific demographic and/or psychographic characteristics of the target group.
    ☐ Establish the numerical size of the target group.
☐ Determine the target market.
    ☐ Establish geographic and numerical size of the target market.
    ☐ Outline specific characteristics of the target market.
☐ Attempt to determine the types of media to be used in the campaign.
    ☐ Rank the media in terms of their order of importance.
        ☐ Relate the rankings to the desired media, group, and market characteristics.
    ☐ Rate the relative importance of the various media considerations.
    ☐ Begin to eliminate some media that do not meet criteria.
    ☐ Rate the media in terms of their contributions to the marketing, advertising, and media objectives.
    ☐ Establish primary and secondary rankings for the media to be used.
    ☐ Provide specific reasons for using each medium.
☐ Determine the specific abilities of each medium.
    ☐ For each medium, analyze the ability to reach the target group.
    ☐ For each medium, analyze the ability to reach the target market.
    ☐ For each medium, estimate the size of audience.
    ☐ For each medium, estimate the effective reach to prospects.
    ☐ For each medium, estimate the quality of audience.
    ☐ For each medium, estimate the cost efficiencies.
☐ Ascertain that all media objectives (as well as marketing and advertising objectives) can be met with the media that have been selected.
☐ Evaluate the environment of the media.
☐ List the media that are not to be used.
    ☐ Provide specific reasons for not using each medium.
☐ Consider merchandising and other promotional support that will be required.
☐ Outline needs for continuity.
    ☐ Relate continuity to timing of the advertising effort.
        ☐ Establish periods of introductory and sustaining phases.
        ☐ Examine needs and uses of flight and hiatus periods.
☐ Develop contingency plans to meet unexpected occurrences.
    ☐ Develop specific action to be taken if sales expectations are not being met.
    ☐ Develop specific action to be taken if a competitor takes some unexpected action.
    ☐ Develop specific action to be taken if sales expectations are being exceeded.
☐ Check back to marketing, advertising, and media objectives to be certain that all objectives can be met with these plans.
☐ Write an executive summary or overview that will go at the beginning of the media plan.

Tactics
☐ Outline specific goals and uses for each medium to be used.
☐ Consider cost efficiencies of each medium.
☐ Select specific media vehicles.
    ☐ Rank the vehicles in terms of their order of importance and applicability.
        ☐ Relate the rankings to the desired media, group, and market characteristics.
    ☐ Consider cost efficiencies of each vehicle.
        ☐ Relate vehicle audiences to anticipated sales levels.
    ☐ Begin to eliminate some vehicles that do not fit the desired pattern.
    ☐ Relate the remaining vehicles to goals, applicability, media environment, targets, and the like.
    ☐ Review competitive considerations.
    ☐ Provide specific reasons for using each vehicle.
    ☐ Establish rankings of the vehicles in their order of use.

☐ Select the units of advertising to be used.
    ☐ Relate the units to the creative considerations.
    ☐ Relate the units to the budgetary considerations.
    ☐ Relate the units to availability of desired units and vehicles and media.
    ☐ Relate the units to cost efficiencies.
☐ Estimate the cost of vehicles and units to be used.
    ☐ Work out various possible arrangements of vehicles and units.
    ☐ Utilize process of elimination until most satisfactory pattern is decided upon.
☐ Check on actual costs of vehicles and units.
    ☐ Compare actual costs to estimates.
    ☐ Make adjustments as necessary.
☐ Check on availability of units and vehicles.
☐ Relate availability to units selected and estimates.
☐ Reserve desired media time and/or space.
☐ Order appropriate time and/or space.
☐ Schedule units of advertising on specific advertising vehicles.
☐ Report plans to client, traffic department, creative department, account management, media representatives, and so on, as appropriate.
    ☐ Report coordination requirements to appropriate departments and personnel.

Advertising Media

The major advertising media include newspaper, television, direct marketing, radio and a variety of other media. The list below provides a breakdown (in alphabetical order) of these media, the total advertising expenditures for which can be found in Figure 2.

Business Publications—Trade papers, professional and industrial publications

Consumer Magazines—General purpose, special interest, and hobby publications

Direct Marketing—Direct mail, telemarketing, and online advertising

Farm Publications—Magazines (often business/consumer hybrids) that target farmers

Newspapers—Dailies, weeklies, special interest, and foreign language newspaper

Outdoor—Billboards and signs

Radio—Network, spot

Specialty Advertising—Calendars, imprinted desk items, and similar give-aways

Television—Broadcast (network and local stations), cable, home videos

Various Others (Miscellaneous)—Transit, point-of-purchase, and all other media

FIGURE 2.
ESTIMATES OF EXPENDITURES IN U.S. ADVERTISING MEDIA

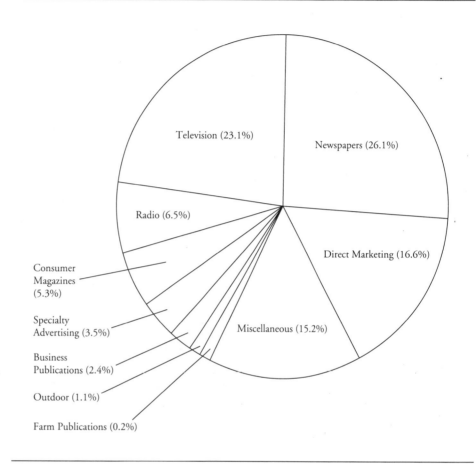

Projections are based on figures from the Newspaper Advertising Bureau, Inc.

S·E·C·T·I·O·N O·N·E

Marketing and Media Research Sources

This section includes representative sources of data and information for each of the major applications in the media process. The applications are: marketing sources, audience research sources, media pricing tables, and media reach estimates.

This is a representative sampling of the available sources. In cases where there are competing research companies, only one was selected. Inclusion is not intended to suggest greater value or accuracy than the others.

Marketing sources contribute to setting of goals and objectives as they investigate competitor activity, consumer brand preferences, and market area profiles.

Audience research sources provide standard measures of audiences of major media. These reports are syndicated; they can be licensed for use by advertisers, agencies, and the media. Custom audience studies are also done, but are exclusively the property of the client organization. All sources in this book are available to any subscriber.

To illustrate cost and price estimators using media pricing tables, a sample of cost estimators used by planners was combined with vehicle rates used by media buyers. Estimators are employed to set budgets and allocations; rate schedules are used for contract negotiation.

Media reach research is used in estimating the unduplicated audience for a specific vehicle or set of vehicles. To better demonstrate a wider perspective, the sources used here are those for planning purposes. Generic estimates are vital in planning stages when the advertising vehicles have not yet been identified.

All the source illustrations in this book are hard-copy reproductions. This is still the most popular format for media data and information, but this is changing.

Throughout our investigations we found virtually every research company offers alternative formats. By the fifth edition of this book, we will be compelled to illustrate the formats for personal computers or work stations. The 21st century will show paper replaced by on-line access, tape cassette, or CD-ROM. Hard copy may be obtained via computer "print-screen" commands.

MEDIA/MARKETING SOURCES
1. Mediamark Research Inc. Marketing Data
2. Sales and Marketing Management Survey of Buying Power
3. Editor and Publisher Market Guide
4. LNA/MediaWatch Multi-Media Service
5. Leading National Advertisers (LNA) Newspaper Spending

MEDIA AUDIENCE MEASUREMENT SOURCES
6. Nielsen National Television Audience Estimates
7. Nielsen Station Index (NSI) Audience Estimates for Local Market Television
8. Arbitron Radio Local Market Reports

9. Simmons Market Research Bureau (SMRB) Demographic Status of Adult Magazine Readers
10. Standard Rate and Data Service (SRDS) Newspaper Circulation Analysis (*Circulation '95*)

MEDIA COST SOURCES AND ESTIMATORS
11. Network Television Cost Estimator
12. Cable Television Network Cost Estimator
13. Spot Television Cost Estimator
14. Network Radio Cost Estimators
15. Spot Market Radio Cost Estimators
16. Daily Newspaper Cost and Coverage Estimator
17. Standard Rate and Data Service (SRDS) Newspaper Rates and Data
18. Standard Rate and Data Service (SRDS) Consumer Magazine and Agri-Media Rates and Data
19. Standard Rate and Data Service (SRDS) Spot Television Rates and Data
20. Outdoor Billboard (Thirty-Sheet) Cost Estimator

MEDIA AUDIENCE REACH ESTIMATORS
21. Spot Market Television Audience Reach Estimator
22. Network Radio Reach and Frequency Estimator
23. Spot Market Radio Audience Reach Estimator
24. Daily Newspaper Multiple Issue Reach Estimator
25. Simmons Market Research Bureau (SMRB) Twelve Issue Reach and Average Frequency (Publications)
26. Simmons Market Research Bureau (SMRB) Duplication of Average Issue Audiences (Publications)
27. Outdoor Posters: Adult Reach Estimator

Source 1
Mediamark Research Inc. (MRI)

Research Company Mediamark Research Inc.

Description Each year more than 20,000 adults are interviewed to learn of their use of product and service categories. Part of the interview also involves a comprehensive examination of social and economic characteristics of each household. Together, these databases provide marketers with a valuable profile of target markets.

Function Because Mediamark studies individual brands' consumers as well as profiles for the complete category, profile comparisons (for all brands) are possible. Blending these demographic data with actual sales patterns for a brand gives managers a better picture of what is happening in the marketplace, and who is doing it. More specifically, these data assist in market allocation decisions, and in media selection.

Format Notes These national surveys try to provide both qualitative and quantitative measures of consumer usage. These dimensions are reflected in the four-column arrangement that is standard in such reports.

    The excerpt shown covers adult women's use of the regular cola soft drink category.

"Total U.S." This first column on the left is the total population estimate for each of the demographic and geographic segments. Total population includes all users and non-users of the product.

"A Column." For all degrees of cola usage, this column estimates the number total of females. The "All" section counts every level of cola drinker; the remaining sections are keyed to heavy, medium, and light drinkers.

"B Column." This converts the raw figures in "A" into a percentage. Thus, this answers what percent of adult female drinkers are this age, or income, or marital status.

"C Column." The statistic in column "C" has a qualitative nature. It shows what percent of U.S. total population (including non-drinkers) consumes cola by level of consumption. Thus, this answers what percent of adult females this age, or income, or marital status are cola drinkers in some form. Note also the very top of the "C" column is the percentage based on all women regardless of demographic status. This allows some comparison with the "average woman" regardless of demographic classification.

"D Column." Is called an index ("INDX") because it compares two percentages; one for the "average" woman, the other for each demographic segment. Indices created by dividing the average percentage into the segment percentage suggest a comparative quality of the segment. An index of 100 is considered average. As indices climb above 100 you are more likely to find a cola drinker than you would from a random group of drinkers.

Illustration Follow one segment across the "Heavy" consumption level. Use "Age 18–24." Mediamark estimates there are 12,395,000 women in this range in the United States. Of that age, 2,643,000 are heavy consumers of cola (Column A). Column B says that 20 percent of heavy cola consumers are 18–24. Column C says that 21.3 percent of women 18–24 are heavy consumers. The index of 158 tells us we are much more likely to find an 18–24 heavy consumer of cola than we would from the average of all age segments.

142 REGULAR COLA DRINKS, NOT DIET

DRINKS OR GLASSES/LAST 7 DAYS

BASE: WOMEN	TOTAL U.S. '000	ALL A '000	B % DOWN	C % ACROSS	D INDEX	HEAVY MORE THAN 7 A '000	B % DOWN	C % ACROSS	D INDEX	MEDIUM 3-7 A '000	B % DOWN	C % ACROSS	D INDEX	LIGHT LESS THAN 3 A '000	B % DOWN	C % ACROSS	D INDEX
All Women	98070	52646	100.0	53.7	100	13212	100.0	13.5	100	18961	100.0	19.3	100	20473	100.0	20.9	100
Household Heads	37747	18982	36.1	50.3	94	4972	37.6	13.2	98	6962	36.7	18.4	95	7048	34.4	18.7	89
Homemakers	86474	45878	87.1	53.1	99	11750	88.9	13.6	101	16174	85.3	18.7	97	17954	87.7	20.8	99
Graduated College	17172	7749	14.7	45.1	84	1333	10.1	7.8	58	2603	13.7	15.2	78	3814	18.6	22.2	106
Attended College	24213	12808	24.3	52.9	99	3103	23.5	12.8	95	4456	23.5	18.4	95	5249	25.6	21.7	104
Graduated High School	36470	21033	40.0	57.7	107	5455	41.3	15.0	111	7998	42.2	21.9	113	7581	37.0	20.8	100
Did not Graduate High School	20215	11055	21.0	54.7	102	3321	25.1	16.4	122	3904	20.6	19.3	100	3829	18.7	18.9	91
18-24	12395	8307	15.8	67.0	125	2643	20.0	21.3	158	3238	17.1	26.1	135	2426	11.8	19.6	94
25-34	21940	13800	26.2	62.9	117	3701	28.0	16.9	125	5039	26.6	23.0	119	5060	24.7	23.1	110
35-44	20374	11346	21.6	55.7	104	3106	23.5	15.2	113	3648	19.2	17.9	93	4593	22.4	22.5	108
45-54	13905	7158	13.6	51.5	96	1462	11.1	10.5	78	2703	14.3	19.4	101	2993	14.6	21.5	103
55-64	11363	5362	10.2	47.2	88	1044	7.9	9.2	68	1730	9.1	15.2	79	2588	12.6	22.8	109
65 or over	18093	6672	12.7	36.9	69	1256	9.5	6.9	52	2602	13.7	14.4	74	2814	13.7	15.6	75
18-34	34335	22107	42.0	64.4	120	6344	48.0	18.5	137	8277	43.7	24.1	125	7486	36.6	21.8	104
18-49	62309	37317	70.9	59.9	112	10329	78.2	16.6	123	13155	69.4	21.1	109	13834	67.6	22.2	106
25-54	56218	32305	61.4	57.5	107	8268	62.6	14.7	109	11391	60.1	20.3	105	12646	61.8	22.5	108
Employed Full Time	42852	23764	45.1	55.5	103	5878	44.5	13.7	102	8395	44.3	19.6	101	9491	46.4	22.1	106
Part-time	11068	6049	11.5	54.7	102	1326	10.0	12.0	89	2327	12.3	21.0	109	2396	11.7	21.6	104
Sole Wage Earner	12891	6623	12.6	51.4	96	1925	14.6	14.9	111	2430	12.8	18.9	97	2268	11.1	17.6	84
Not Employed	44149	22833	43.4	51.7	96	6008	45.5	13.6	101	8239	43.5	18.7	97	8586	41.9	19.4	93
Professional	8987	4302	8.2	47.9	89	935	7.1	10.4	77	1422	7.5	15.8	82	1945	9.5	21.6	104
Executive/Admin./Managerial	6554	3279	6.2	50.0	93	*388	2.9	5.9	44	1120	5.9	17.1	88	1771	8.7	27.0	129
Clerical/Sales/Technical	23136	13193	25.1	57.0	106	3309	25.0	14.3	106	4445	23.4	19.2	99	5439	26.6	23.5	113
Precision/Crafts/Repair	1153	574	1.1	49.8	93	*158	1.2	13.7	102	*246	1.3	21.3	110	*171	.8	14.8	71
Other Employed	14091	8464	16.1	60.1	112	2414	18.3	17.1	127	3489	18.4	24.8	128	2561	12.5	18.2	87
H/D Income $75,000 or More	12070	5537	10.5	45.9	85	960	7.3	8.0	59	1779	9.4	14.7	76	2798	13.7	23.2	111
$60,000 - 74,999	8061	4051	7.7	50.3	94	663	5.0	8.2	61	1302	6.9	16.2	84	2086	10.2	25.9	124
$50,000 - 59,999	8792	4505	8.6	51.2	95	925	7.0	10.5	78	1629	8.6	18.5	96	1952	9.5	22.2	106
$40,000 - 49,999	10989	6151	11.7	56.0	104	1551	11.7	14.1	105	2273	12.0	20.7	107	2327	11.4	21.2	101
$30,000 - 39,999	13588	7989	15.2	58.8	110	2078	15.7	15.3	114	2954	15.6	21.7	112	2957	14.4	21.8	104
$20,000 - 29,999	15576	9133	17.3	58.6	109	2406	18.2	15.4	115	3313	17.5	21.3	110	3413	16.7	21.9	105
$10,000 - 19,999	16276	8393	15.9	51.6	96	2466	18.7	15.2	112	3315	17.5	20.4	105	2611	12.8	16.0	77
Less than $10,000	12718	6888	13.1	54.2	101	2164	16.4	17.0	126	2395	12.6	18.8	97	2329	11.4	18.3	88
Census Region: North East	20976	10566	20.1	50.4	94	2293	17.4	10.9	81	3672	19.4	17.5	91	4601	22.5	21.9	105
North Central	23354	12298	23.4	52.7	98	3067	23.2	13.1	97	4456	23.5	19.1	99	4775	23.3	20.4	98
South	33856	20278	38.5	59.9	112	5935	44.9	17.5	130	7677	40.5	22.7	117	6665	32.6	19.7	94
West	19883	9504	18.1	47.8	89	1916	14.5	9.6	72	3155	16.6	15.9	82	4433	21.7	22.3	107
Marketing Reg.: New England	5487	2386	4.5	43.5	81	*493	3.7	9.0	67	661	3.5	12.0	62	1231	6.0	22.4	107
Middle Atlantic	17680	9365	17.8	53.0	99	2031	15.4	11.5	85	3620	19.1	20.5	106	3715	18.1	21.0	101
East Central	13338	7545	14.3	56.6	105	2111	16.0	15.8	117	2774	14.6	20.8	108	2660	13.0	19.9	96
West Central	14950	7582	14.4	50.7	94	1876	14.2	12.5	93	2548	13.4	17.0	88	3157	15.4	21.1	101
South East	18443	10991	20.9	59.6	111	3531	26.7	19.1	142	4306	22.7	23.3	121	3154	15.4	17.1	82
South West	10759	6478	12.3	60.2	112	1582	12.0	14.7	109	2250	11.9	20.9	108	2646	12.9	24.6	118
Pacific	17412	8299	15.8	47.7	89	1588	12.0	9.1	68	2801	14.8	16.1	83	3910	19.1	22.5	108
County Size A	40327	20226	38.4	50.2	93	4046	30.6	10.0	74	7411	39.1	18.4	95	8770	42.8	21.7	104
County Size B	29240	16826	32.0	57.5	107	4829	36.6	16.5	123	5862	30.9	20.0	104	6135	30.0	21.0	101
County Size C	14036	7723	14.7	55.0	102	2314	17.5	16.5	122	2767	14.6	19.7	102	2642	12.9	18.8	90
County Size D	14466	7870	14.9	54.4	101	2023	15.3	14.0	104	2920	15.4	20.2	104	2927	14.3	20.2	97
MSA Central City	35097	18909	35.9	53.9	100	5173	39.2	14.7	109	6794	35.8	19.4	100	6943	33.9	19.8	95
MSA Suburban	41787	22177	42.1	53.1	99	5083	38.5	12.2	90	7702	40.6	18.4	95	9391	45.9	22.5	108
Non-MSA	21185	11560	22.0	54.6	102	2956	22.4	14.0	104	4465	23.5	21.1	109	4139	20.2	19.5	94
Single	18619	11303	21.5	60.7	113	3308	25.0	17.8	132	4209	22.2	22.6	117	3787	18.5	20.3	97
Married	55399	29651	56.3	53.5	100	7096	53.7	12.8	95	10487	55.3	18.9	98	12068	58.9	21.8	104
Other	24051	11691	22.2	48.6	91	2808	21.3	11.7	87	4265	22.5	17.7	92	4618	22.6	19.2	92
Parents	36667	22552	42.8	61.5	115	6293	47.6	17.2	127	7968	42.0	21.7	112	8291	40.5	22.6	108
Working Parents	23298	13879	26.4	59.6	111	3425	25.9	14.7	109	5036	26.6	21.6	112	5418	26.5	23.3	111
Household Size: 1 Person	14545	6128	11.6	42.1	78	1229	9.3	8.4	63	2211	11.7	15.2	79	2689	13.1	18.5	89
2 Persons	29698	14269	27.1	48.0	90	3511	26.6	11.8	88	5233	27.6	17.6	91	5524	27.0	18.6	89
3 or More	53827	32249	61.3	59.9	112	8472	64.1	15.7	117	11517	60.7	21.4	111	12260	59.9	22.8	109
Any Child in Household	42507	26177	49.7	61.6	115	7215	54.6	17.0	126	9271	48.9	21.8	113	9691	47.3	22.8	109
Under 2 Years	8925	5876	11.2	65.8	123	1677	12.7	18.8	139	2075	10.9	23.2	120	2124	10.4	23.8	114
2-5 Years	17040	11116	21.1	65.2	122	3122	23.6	18.3	136	4121	21.7	24.2	125	3873	18.9	22.7	109
6-11 Years	18928	11494	21.8	60.7	113	3309	25.0	17.5	130	4207	22.2	22.2	115	3978	19.4	21.0	101
12-17 Years	18055	10834	20.6	60.0	112	2731	20.7	15.1	112	3613	19.1	20.0	104	4490	21.9	24.9	119
White	82977	43006	81.7	51.8	97	10080	76.3	12.1	90	15553	82.0	18.7	97	17372	84.9	20.9	100
Black	11661	7617	14.5	65.3	122	2669	20.2	22.9	170	2716	14.3	23.3	120	2232	10.9	19.1	92
Spanish Speaking	6577	3918	7.4	59.6	111	841	6.4	12.8	95	1534	8.1	23.3	121	1543	7.5	23.5	112
Home Owned	65954	33615	63.9	51.0	95	7653	57.9	11.6	86	11757	62.0	17.8	92	14206	69.4	21.5	103

Source 2
Survey of Buying Power

· ·

Research Company   *Sales and Marketing Management* magazine

Description   This is a traditional source for statewide demographic and sales figures. The data are compiled from federal and state census work. This data is updated yearly and the magazine publishes the *Survey* each fall.

Function   This data is best used for geographic comparisons of markets. It can assist in evaluating areas for product introduction, roll-outs, or test markets. Much of its demographic data is also used in customized sales indices such as brand or category development indexing.

Format Notes   Two of the statistics prepared for the *Survey* are somewhat unusual and deserve explanation.

"**Effective Buying Income.**"   This per household figure includes all sources of income from any member *less* taxes and Social Security payments.

"**Buying Power Index.**"   This is a comparative index constructed from an area's population, effective buying income, and total retail sales. By calculating the percentage of the United States for each statistic and giving each a weighting factor, the magazine is able to assign a vitality index for every metropolitan area in the 50 states. The *Survey* encourages marketers to create customized indices that reflect more targeted age segments, income sets, and specialized retail markets.

METRO & COUNTY TOTALS

New Mexico

S&MM ESTIMATES:

POPULATION / RETAIL SALES BY STORE GROUP

METRO AREA / County / City	Total Population (Thousands)	% Of U.S.	Median Age Of Pop.	18-24 Years	25-34 Years	35-49 Years	50 & Over	House-holds (Thousands)	Total Retail Sales ($000)	Food ($000)	Eating & Drinking Places ($000)	General Mdse. ($000)	Furniture/ Furnish. Appliance ($000)	Auto-motive ($000)	Drug ($000)
ALBUQUERQUE	653.3	.2491	33.0	8.9	17.0	23.7	22.8	246.3	6,239,500	1,100,271	809,392	888,074	390,539	1,427,122	192,337
Bernalillo	520.0	.1983	33.3	9.4	17.0	24.0	23.1	201.7	5,690,250	935,790	728,904	833,781	375,477	1,335,826	168,641
•Albuquerque	413.6	.1577	33.6	9.8	17.2	23.9	23.7	166.1	5,372,723	866,159	663,106	810,222	372,131	1,304,825	150,593
Sandoval	78.1	.0298	31.2	6.8	17.2	22.9	20.6	26.1	239,820	84,828	47,293	23,584	9,950	8,205	13,260
Valencia	55.2	.0210	32.3	7.4	15.4	23.0	22.9	18.5	309,430	79,653	33,195	30,709	5,112	83,091	10,436
SUBURBAN TOTAL	239.7	.0914	31.7	7.5	16.3	23.4	21.3	80.2	866,777	234,112	146,286	77,852	18,408	122,297	41,744
LAS CRUCES	157.3	.0600	28.8	13.0	15.5	19.8	20.6	52.0	1,006,383	204,308	138,513	132,061	46,878	186,566	24,910
Dona Ana	157.3	.0600	28.8	13.0	15.5	19.8	20.6	52.0	1,006,383	204,308	138,513	132,061	46,878	186,566	24,910
•Las Cruces	70.4	.0268	31.3	12.8	15.9	19.8	24.3	26.7	910,319	183,503	111,763	123,982	46,122	179,193	24,760
SUBURBAN TOTAL	86.9	.0332	26.6	13.2	15.1	19.8	17.5	25.3	96,064	20,805	26,750	8,079	756	7,373	150
SANTA FE	132.7	.0506	36.0	7.3	14.6	28.2	23.8	51.4	1,566,662	247,575	256,541	153,228	126,392	244,310	34,390
Los Alamos	18.6	.0071	38.9	4.4	12.5	29.7	27.5	7.5	90,593	43,659	15,940	3,258	1,691	143	1,961
Santa Fe	114.1	.0435	35.6	7.8	14.9	28.0	23.2	43.9	1,476,069	203,916	240,601	149,970	124,701	244,167	32,429
•Santa Fe	63.6	.0243	37.2	8.5	14.2	27.6	26.6	26.0	1,427,461	197,857	232,486	149,775	122,999	241,459	32,209
SUBURBAN TOTAL	69.1	.0263	35.0	6.3	14.9	28.7	21.3	25.4	139,201	49,718	24,055	3,453	3,393	2,851	2,181

EFFECTIVE BUYING INCOME

% of Hslds. by EBI Group:
(A) $10,000-$19,999
(B) $20,000-$34,999
(C) $35,000-$49,999
(D) $50,000 & Over

METRO AREA / County / City	Total EBI ($000)	Median Hsld. EBI	A	B	C	D	Buying Power Index
ALBUQUERQUE	10,368,112	34,696	15.9	23.4	19.3	30.3	.2501
Bernalillo	8,432,384	33,978	16.3	23.9	18.7	29.7	.2108
•Albuquerque	6,922,088	34,308	16.6	22.9	19.0	30.1	.1815
Sandoval	1,222,509	42,316	11.6	19.8	22.5	38.4	.0229
Valencia	713,219	31,873	17.4	24.2	20.6	24.8	.0164
SUBURBAN TOTAL	3,446,024	35,487	14.4	24.3	19.9	30.8	.0686
LAS CRUCES	1,715,974	26,310	21.6	24.7	16.9	19.6	.0447
Dona Ana	1,715,974	26,310	21.6	24.7	16.9	19.6	.0447
•Las Cruces	910,494	28,264	19.3	22.3	18.3	21.8	.0278
SUBURBAN TOTAL	805,480	24,656	24.0	27.4	15.4	17.2	.0169
SANTA FE	2,644,412	40,828	13.0	21.3	17.8	39.6	.0610
Los Alamos	517,881	67,233	5.7	10.3	13.3	68.0	.0085
Santa Fe	2,126,531	37,400	14.2	23.2	18.5	34.8	.0525
•Santa Fe	1,275,647	38,273	14.1	22.1	18.8	35.6	.0383
SUBURBAN TOTAL	1,368,765	43,969	11.9	20.6	16.6	43.8	.0227
OTHER COUNTIES							
Catron	23,546	21,000	24.8	32.1	12.9	7.1	.0005
Chaves	751,291	26,296	20.8	26.5	17.3	17.9	.0192
Roswell	604,821	26,574	20.1	26.0	17.1	18.8	.0164
Cibola	201,421	21,307	24.0	25.4	14.9	12.3	.0061
Colfax	186,695	28,189	21.5	24.8	18.9	20.3	.0048
Curry	565,219	26,201	21.9	29.1	16.7	18.3	.0150
De Baca	24,712	20,612	29.0	24.9	15.4	11.0	.0006
Eddy	686,616	29,948	17.6	24.2	18.5	23.8	.0166
Grant	340,547	26,940	20.6	26.9	19.0	17.7	.0085
Guadalupe	34,122	16,556	27.9	22.9	12.6	6.0	.0013
Harding	11,667	23,113	25.0	31.8	12.4	14.0	.0002
Hidalgo	77,765	30,637	18.5	20.1	22.8	23.0	.0019
Lea	681,704	28,942	18.4	24.0	19.1	21.7	.0174
Lincoln	192,101	24,656	23.4	24.4	16.1	18.4	.0052
Luna	192,832	18,103	29.1	25.0	11.0	8.7	.0058
McKinley	523,857	22,392	19.3	22.6	15.0	16.6	.0189
Mora	40,191	17,360	26.2	24.8	6.1	12.5	.0012
Otero	699,179	29,649	18.5	30.3	18.8	21.1	.0163
Quay	105,379	20,212	24.2	25.8	14.3	10.4	.0033
Rio Arriba	336,098	22,032	24.4	24.9	14.9	14.3	.0094
Roosevelt	197,197	21,750	24.2	24.1	15.6	13.9	.0052
San Juan	1,001,486	26,526	18.7	23.3	18.2	19.5	.0304
San Miguel	272,723	22,731	22.7	25.3	15.5	14.5	.0078
Sierra	140,137	21,167	26.9	26.5	14.0	11.9	.0033
Socorro	183,161	24,956	20.3	21.0	16.8	20.2	.0044
Taos	260,918	19,838	25.8	25.5	12.2	11.9	.0080
Torrance	132,588	24,452	23.3	26.1	17.3	15.9	.0031
Union	51,348	21,218	26.8	20.4	15.2	16.7	.0012
TOTAL METRO COUNTIES	14,728,498	34,153	16.3	23.4	18.7	30.0	.3558
TOTAL STATE	22,642,998	30,032	18.3	24.2	17.9	24.8	.5714

Source 3
Editor and Publisher Market Guide

Research Company *Editor and Publisher* magazine

Description The *Editor and Publisher Market Guide* is produced by the magazine held to be the leading trade magazine for the newspaper industry. This gives it a natural access to local market information. Each local newspaper assists in the compilation of municipal, utility, banking, and retail information to provide a standardized profile.

Function Used in concert with other databases such as *Survey of Buying Power* in Source 2, the *Guide* adds a wealth of descriptive detail. For small cities and towns, it is probably unique in its scope. The *Market Guide* fulfills diverse needs of marketers: retail distribution, identification of geographic locations from rail and highway access, and provision of support data for sales analysis.

Format Notes States and population centers are arranged alphabetically. Each listing covers 15 topics for marketing and a newspaper listing.

Population and household estimates are based upon the 1990 Census, but are updated annually from local sources.

The population estimates shown as ''CZ-ABC'' and ''RTZ-ABC'' refer to city zone and retail trading zone as determined by the Audit Bureau of Circulation, the newspaper industry's ''accountant'' for circulation.

Local Contact: for Advertising and Merchandising Data: Connie Nuese, Adv. Mgr., INDEPENDENT, Box 411, Marshall, MN 56258; Tel. (507) 537-1551, FAX (507) 537-1557.
National Representatives: Minnesota Newspaper Association; Papert Companies.

MINNEAPOLIS

1 - LOCATION: Hennepin County (In Minneapolis-St. Paul, MN-WI MSA), E&P Map C-4. County Seat. Transportation center for MN, ND, SD and 16 counties in western WI; industrial and wholesale center of the upper Midwest area. In east central part of state; 419 mi. from Chicago, 351 mi. from Milwaukee; 355 mi. from Omaha, 459 mi. from Winnipeg. On U.S. Interstate Freeways 35, 394, 494 and 694; Hwys. 10, 12, 52 61, 169 & 212; State Hwys. 5, 7, 36, 47, 51, 55, 56, 95, 120, 149, 152, 190 & 242.

2 - TRANSPORTATION: Railroads: Amtrak; Milwaukee Road; Burlington Northern; Soo Line; Chicago & NorthWestern; Norfolk Southern; Southern Pacific; Union Pacific.
Motor Freight Carriers: Over 100 truck lines.
Intercity Bus Lines: Greyhound; Jefferson; Zephyr.
Airlines: American; America West; Bear Skin; Continental; Delta; Express Two; Great Lakes Aviation; KLM; Mesaba; Northwest; Sun Country; TWA; United; USAir; Canadian Regional.

3 - POPULATION:
Corp. City 90 Cen. 368,383; E&P 95 Est. 366,469
County 90 Cen. 1,032,431; E&P 95 Est. 1,102,062
MSA 90 Cen. 2,538,834; E&P 95 Est. 2,780,035
NDM-ABC: (90) 2,579,160

4 - HOUSEHOLDS:
Corp. City 90 Cen. 142,186; E&P 95 Est. 141,447
County 90 Cen. 412,972; E&P 95 Est. 440,824
MSA 90 Cen. 1,078,611; E&P 95 Est. 1,190,224
NDM-ABC: (90) 974,540

5 - BANKS	NUMBER	DEPOSITS
Commercial	195	$23,144,400,000
Savings & Loan	8	$3,261,052,000

6 - PASSENGER AUTOS: Hennepin County 640,301

7 - ELECTRIC METERS: Residence 522,647

8 - GAS METERS: Residence 415,000

9 - PRINCIPAL INDUSTRIES: Industry, No. of Wage Earners (Av. Wkly. Wage)- Health Services 105,000 ; Wholesale Trade 5,700 ($515); Eating & Drinking Places 83,800 ($143); Business Services 92,100; Transportation 54,300; Industrial Machinery Manufacturing 49,900 ($594); Insurance 42,200; Finance 43,500; General Merchandise 37,700 ($255); Printing and Publishing 37,400 ($490).

10 - CLIMATE: Min. & Max. Temp.- Spring 36-55; Summer 61-82; Fall 39-61; Winter 9-26 First Killing Frost Oct. 8; Last Killing Frost Apr. 29.

11 - TAP WATER: Alkaline, soft; fluoridated. In suburbs (400,000 people) hard.

12 - RETAILING: Principal Shopping Center- 8 blocks on Hennepin, Nicollet and Marquette Aves.
Neighborhood Shopping Centers- Apache Plaza; Apple Valley Sq.; Bandana Square; Bonaventure; Brandon Sq.; Brickyard; Brighton Village; Broadway Center; Brookdale Sq.; Brookview Plaza; Butler Sq.; Burhaven Mall; Burnhill Plaza; Burnside Plaza; Calhoun Sq.; Calhoun Village; Cedarvale; Central Plaza; Centra; Valu Ctr.; Champlin Plaza; Cherokee Ctr.; City Center; Cliff Lake Ctr.; Clover Ctr.; Cobblestone Court; Colonial Sq.; Columbia Heights Mall; The Commons; Conservatory; Coon Rapids Family Ctr.; Coon Rapids Village Ctr.; Cottage Sq.; Country Village; Crystal; Crystal Gallery; Diamondhead Mall; Down Town Center; Eagan Town Ctr.; Edinburgh; Fairdale Shoppes; Four Seasons Mall; Franklin Circle Ctr.; Galleria; Galtier Plaza; Gaviidae Plaza; Glenhaven Ctr.; Grove Plaza; Grove Sq.; Hamline Ctr.; Har Mar Mall; Highland; Highland Village; Hi-Lake;

Hillcrest; Holly Center; Hub; Jerry's; Keller Lake Ctr.; Knollwood; Knollwood Village; Leisure Lane; Lillydale; Loehmann's Plaza; Manufacturer's Market; Maple Grove Mall; Mapleridge Ctr.; Marina Ctr.; The Market Place; Market Plaza; Market Square; Menard's Plaza; Mendota Plaza; Midland; Midtown; Midway; Minnehaha Mall; Minnesota Valley Mall; Miracle Mile; Moore Lake Commons; Mounds View Sq.; Normandale; Northbrook Ctr.; Northcourt Commons; Northdale Ctr.; Northgate Mall; Northway; Northwind Plaza; Oakdale Mall; Oxboro Ctr.; Park Plaza; Park Square; Pavillion Place; Phalen; Pioneer Village; Plaza 94; Plaza 3000; Plymouth Plaza; Prairieview Ctr.; Prairie Village Mall; Preserve Village; Priordale Mall; Rainbow Plaza; Rice Creek; Richfield Shoppes; Ridgehaven; RidgeSquare North; River Heights Plaza; Riverplace; Robert Sq.; Robin Ctr.; Robbinsdale Town Ctr.; Rosedale Sq.; St. Anthony Main; St. Croix Mall; 7-Hi; Shannon Sq.; Shingle Creek Ctr.; Sibley Plaza; Signal Hills; Skywood Mall; Southdale Shops; Southdale Sq.; South Fork; Southridge Ctr.; Southtown; Southview; Southview Mall; Springbrook Mall; Star Plaza; Suburban Sq.; Sun Ray; Terrace Mall; Texa-Tonka; Town and Country Sq.; Town Center; Town Sq.; Unidale; Valley Creek Mall; Valley Plaza; Valley Ridge; Valley West; Village North; Village Sq.; Village Ten; Wayzata Bay Ctr.; Westbrooke Mall; West View Mall; Westview Valu Ctr.; Westwind Plaza; Winnetka Ctr.; Yankee Doodle Sq.; Yorkdale Shoppes; Yorktown Mall; Zachary Sq.; Zanebrook.

Nearby Shopping Centers

Name (No. of stores)	Miles from Downtown	Principal Stores
Brookdale (82)	6	JCPenney, Dayton's, Sears, Carson Pirie Scott
Burnsville Center (170)	18	Carson Pirie Scott, JCPenney, Dayton's, Sears
Eden Prairie Center (88)	18	Carson Pirie Scott, Target, Sears
Mall of America	7	Nordstrom, Bloomingdale's, Sears, Macy's
Maplewood Mall (150)	10	Carson Pirie Scott, Kohl's, Sears
Northtown (115)	11	Kohl's, Montgomery Ward, Carson Pirie Scott
Ridgedale (140)	9	JCPenney, Carson Pirie Scott, Dayton's, Sears
Rosedale (164)	5	Dayton's, Carson Pirie Scott, Montgomery Ward, JCPenney
Southdale (180)	7	Carson Pirie Scott, JCPenney, Dayton's

Stores Open Evenings- Mon. to Fri.; Food & Dept.

13 - RETAIL OUTLETS: Department Stores- Dayton's (7); Carson Pirie Scott (10); JCPenney (8); Sears (9); Saks Fifth Avenue; Neiman Marcus; Bloomingdale's; Macy's, Nordstrom; Kohl's (6); Herberger's (3).
Discount Stores- Target (28); K mart (20); Holiday Plus (4); Wal-Mart (9); Marshalls; T.J. Maxx; Montgomery Ward (6).
Variety Store- Woolworth (9).
Chain Supermarkets- Red Owl; Lund's (8); IGA (50); Rainbow (22); 7-Eleven (60); Brooks (12); Country Club (19); Holiday (4); Kenny's Markets (25); Knowlan's (8); PDQ (28); Schiller's (4); Super Valu (35); Tom Thumb (89); Byerly's (8); Cub Foods (9); Thriftway; Star (20); Country Market (9).
Other Chain Stores- Big A; Car Quest; Genuine Parts; Firestone; Coast-to-Coast; Goodrich; Goodyear; Big Wheel; Champion; 10,000 Auto Parts; NAPA; Connco; Famous Footware; Kinney; Florsheim; Freeman; Bakers;

Burt's; Chandler's; Schuler; Foot Locker; Naturalizer; Payless Shoes; Casual Corner; Brauns; House of Large Sizes; Lane Bryant; Peck & Peck; Liemandts; The Limited; Three Sisters; Shirley's Maternity; Foreman & Clark; Hubert W. White; Brooks Brothers; Lancers; Juster's; Darveaux; Fanny Farmer; Fannie Mae; Bachman's; Frank's; Gabberts; Slumberland; Levitz; Wickes; Schneidermans; Scandinavian Design; Best Buy Co.; Audio King; Radio Shack; Builder's Square; Home Values; OK Hdwe.; Our Own Hdwe.; True Value; Warner Hdwe.; Menard's; Color Tile; Knox; Budget Power; Sherwin-Williams; Bodine's; Schmitt Music; Century Camera; Black Photography; S&L Gen. Mdse.; Minnesota Fabrics; Singer; Mills Fleet Farm Supply (4).

14 - MILITARY INSTALLATIONS: N.A.
15 - COLLEGES AND UNIVERSITIES: University of Minnesota.
16 - NEWSPAPERS: STAR TRIBUNE (m-mon to sat) 412,438; (S) 696,084; ABC Apr. 2,1994.
Local Contact: for Advertising and Merchandising Data: Jim Diaz, Sr. V.P./Gen. Mgr., Marketer Customer Unit, STAR TRIBUNE, 425 Portland Ave., Minneapolis, MN 55488; Tel. (612) 673-4975.
National Representatives: Sawyer-Ferguson-Walker; American Publishers Reps.

MOORHEAD
See FARGO, ND

NEW ULM

1 - LOCATION: Brown County, E&P Map B-4. County Seat. Agricultural center. 97 mi. SW of Twin Cities; 30 mi. W of Mankato; 50 mi. N of Fairmont. On U.S. Hwy. 14; State Hwy. 15.

2 - TRANSPORTATION: Railroads: D.M. & E.
Motor Freight Carriers: 12.
Intercity Bus Line: Jack Rabbit.
Airport: New Ulm Municipal Airport.

3 - POPULATION:
Corp. City 90 Cen. 13,132; E&P 95 Est. 12,684
County 90 Cen. 26,984; E&P 95 Est. 26,283
CZ-ABC: (90) 13,132
RTZ-ABC: (90) 36,923
Total Market: (90) 50,055

4 - HOUSEHOLDS:
Corp. City 90 Cen. 4,811; E&P 95 Est. 4,647
County 90 Cen. 9,782; E&P 95 Est. 9,258
CZ-ABC: (90) 5,199
RTZ-ABC: (90) 13,743
Total Market: (90) 18,942

5 - BANKS	NUMBER	DEPOSITS
Commercial	5	$203,100,000
Savings & Loan	1	$62,100,000

6 - PASSENGER AUTOS: Brown County 16,097

7 - ELECTRIC METERS: Residence 6,339

8 - GAS METERS: Residence 5,015

9 - PRINCIPAL INDUSTRIES: Industry, No. of Wage Earners- Manufacturing 3,911; Trade 2,539; Services 1,984; Construction 470; Government 1,121; Trans. and Util. 580; Finance 404.

10 - CLIMATE: Min. & Max. Temp.- Spring 28-60; Summer 37-99; Fall 33-90; Winter 25-48. First Killing Frost Oct. 1; Last Killing Frost May 4.

11 - TAP WATER: Neutral, hard (495 ppm); fluoridated.

12 - RETAILING: Principal Shopping Centers- 7 blocks on three sts.; shopping ctr. on South side of Town, with Hy-Vee Super Mkt. & Pamida; shopping ctr. on North side of town, Randall Valu Center; Cash Wise Foods; K mart.
Principal Shopping Days- Mon., Wed., Fri., Sat., Sun.
Stores Open Evenings- Mon.; Thur.; Food-daily.

Stores Open Sunday- Specialty shops; Mall; Herbergers; K mart; Pamida; grocery.
Stores Close- 5 pm.

13 - RETAIL OUTLETS: Department Stores- Herberger's; Ehler's; Dueber's.
Discount Stores- Pamida; K mart; Big Bear; Runnings Big R.
Variety Store- Ben Franklin.
Chain Drug Store- Thrifty White.
Chain Supermarkets- Cash Wise; Randall's Super Value; Hy-Vee.
Fast Food/Chain Restaurants- Hardee's; Burger King; McDonald's; KFC; Dairy Queen; Subway.
Auto Dealerships- Bob Schuck Chevrolet (Chevrolet); Jensen Motors (Buick, Olds, Pontiac, Cadillac); Martinka Motors (Chrysler, Plymouth); Pagel Ford (Ford, Lincoln, Mercury).
Other Chain Stores- General Trading; Maurice's; Payless Shoes; Tradehome Shoes; Athletic Fitters; Fashion Bug; Tires Plus; Nina B; Vanity; Goodyear; Midwest Vision Centers.

14 - MILITARY INSTALLATIONS: Installation Name, (Branch)- MN National Guard Armory (Army).

15 - COLLEGES AND UNIVERSITIES: N.A.

16 - NEWSPAPERS: JOURNAL (m-mon to sat) 10,159; (S) 10,560; ABC Mar. 31, 1994.
Local Contact: for Advertising and Merchandising Data: Bruce Fenske, Pub., JOURNAL, 303 N. Minnesota; PO Box 487, New Ulm, MN 56073; Tel. (507) 359-2911.
National Representative: Papert Companies.

NORTH MANKATO
See MANKATO

OWATONNA

1 - LOCATION: Steele County, E&P Map C-4. County Seat. Major manufacturing and shipping center for agricultural area. SE part of state. 60 mi. S of Minneapolis; On U.S. Hwys. 14 & 218; I-35.

2 - TRANSPORTATION: Railroads: C & NW; SooLine; DM & E.
Motor Freight Carriers: 14.
Intercity Bus Line: Jefferson Transportation.
Airport: Owatonna Municipal Airport.

3 - POPULATION:
Corp. City 90 Cen. 19,386; E&P 95 Est. 19,972
County 90 Cen. 30,729; E&P 95 Est. 31,529
CZ-ABC: (90) 19,386
RTZ-ABC: (90) 12,322
Total Market: (90) 31,708

4 - HOUSEHOLDS:
Corp. City 90 Cen. 7,305; E&P 95 Est. 7,526
County 90 Cen. 11,430; E&P 95 Est. 11,728
CZ-ABC: (90) 7,382
RTZ-ABC: (90) 4,306
Total Market: (90) 11,688

5 - BANKS	NUMBER	DEPOSITS
Commercial	5	$303,000,000
Credit Unions	1	$10,000,000

6 - PASSENGER AUTOS: Steele County 18,818

7 - ELECTRIC METERS: Residence 6,985

8 - GAS METERS: Residence 6,457

9 - PRINCIPAL INDUSTRIES: Industry, No. of Wage Earners- Manufacturing 5,529; Insurance 1,040; Government 320; Nursing Home & Hospital 400. Total Wage Earners 16,453.
Principal Pay Days- Wed., Fri.

10 - CLIMATE: Min. & Max. Temp. - Spring 10-97; Summer 54-98; Fall -16-70; Winter -21-61. First Killing Frost Sept. 6; Last Killing Frost Apr. 18.

11 - TAP WATER: Neutral; fluoridated.

12 - RETAILING: Principal Shopping Centers- Downtown, 50 stores; Oakdale, 18 blocks S. of Downtown area on S. Cedar; Cedar Mall, over 10 stores; Medford Outlet, over 40 stores.

Source 4
LNA/MediaWatch Multi-Media Service
....

Research Company   LNA/MediaWatch Competitive Media Reporting

Description   This is a collaborative effort among a number of observation services to provide a summary view of quarterly and year-to-date spending on a national scale. This group covers ten mass media activities.

Function   Tracking the direction and level of competitors is a major preoccupation of marketers of consumer products and services. This particular service gives an overview of most media activity. Other services in competitive reporting cover specifics such as which newspapers and which cities received TV spot. Together, they provide an important surveillance of the marketplace.

Format Notes   This summary is easy to read because most of the detail has been removed. The questions answered are: who spent? how much? which media? and when?

The categories of competition are determined by the service and are compiled under a "Class Code."

The dollars shown are in decimals, but reflect spending in thousands. For example, our excerpt shows the Variety Arts Theatre. The "58.3" in newspaper means $58,300 was spent in the first quarter of 1995.

LNA/MEDIAWATCH MULTI-MEDIA SERVICE
January - June 1995

CLASS/BRAND $

QUARTERLY AND YEAR-TO-DATE ADVERTISING DOLLARS (000)

CLASS/COMPANY/BRAND		CLASS CODE	10-MEDIA TOTAL	MAGAZINES	SUNDAY MAGAZINES	NEWSPAPERS	OUTDOOR	NETWORK TELEVISION	SPOT TELEVISION	SYNDICATED TELEVISION	CABLE TV NETWORKS	NETWORK RADIO	NATIONAL SPOT RADIO
G321 DANCE, THEATER, CONCERTS, OPERA -- CONTINUED													
VARIETY ARTS THEATRE VARIETY ARTS THEATRE	Q1	G321	58.3	---	---	58.3	---	---	---	---	---	---	---
	Q2		35.7	---	---	35.7	---	---	---	---	---	---	---
	95 YTD		94.0	---	---	94.0	---	---	---	---	---	---	---
	94 YTD		29.3	---	---	29.3	---	---	---	---	---	---	---
VICTOR VICTORIA BROADWAY PRODUCTION VICTOR VICTORIA	Q1	G321	80.7	80.7	---	---	---	---	---	---	---	---	---
	95 YTD		80.7	80.7	---	---	---	---	---	---	---	---	---
VICTORIA PALACE THEATRE VICTORIA PALACE THEATRE	Q1	G321	25.3	---	---	---	---	---	25.3	---	---	---	---
	95 YTD		25.3	---	---	---	---	---	25.3	---	---	---	---
WALT DISNEY CO WALT DISNEY PRODUCTIONS STAGE SHOW	Q1	G321	11.0	---	---	---	11.0	---	---	---	---	---	---
	95 YTD		11.0	---	---	---	11.0	---	---	---	---	---	---
WALTER KERR THEATRE WALTER KERR THEATRE	Q1	G321	126.9	2.2	---	124.7	---	---	---	---	---	---	---
	Q2		112.0	---	---	112.0	---	---	---	---	---	---	---
	95 YTD		238.9	2.2	---	236.7	---	---	---	---	---	---	---
	94 YTD		210.0	---	---	210.0	---	---	---	---	---	---	---
WESTWOOD PLAYHOUSE WESTWOOD PLAYHOUSE	Q1	G321	73.3	---	---	73.3	---	---	---	---	---	---	---
	Q2		70.6	---	---	70.6	---	---	---	---	---	---	---
	95 YTD		143.9	---	---	143.9	---	---	---	---	---	---	---
	94 YTD		84.2	---	---	84.2	---	---	---	---	---	---	---
WHAT GOES AROUND COMES AROUND PLAY BROADWAY PROD WHAT GOES AROUND COMES ARD	Q1	G321	202.2	---	---	---	---	---	202.2	---	---	---	---
	Q2		3.1	---	---	---	---	---	3.1	---	---	---	---
	95 YTD		205.3	---	---	---	---	---	205.3	---	---	---	---
WHERE DO I GO FROM HERE BROADWAY PROD WHERE DO I GO FROM HERE	Q1	G321	36.6	---	---	---	---	---	36.6	---	---	---	---
	Q2		25.1	---	---	---	---	---	25.1	---	---	---	---
	95 YTD		61.7	---	---	---	---	---	61.7	---	---	---	---
WHITNEY MUSEUM OF AMERICAN ART WHITNEY MUSEUM OF AMERICAN ART	Q1	G321	8.2	---	---	8.2	---	---	---	---	---	---	---
	Q2		142.8	13.2	51.2	78.4	---	---	---	---	---	---	---
	95 YTD		151.0	13.2	51.2	86.6	---	---	---	---	---	---	---
	94 YTD		26.8	26.8	---	---	---	---	---	---	---	---	---
WILL ROGERS FOLLIES BROADWAY PRODUCTION WILL ROGERS FOLLIES	Q1	G321	179.6	---	---	---	---	---	179.6	---	---	---	---
	Q2		56.1	---	---	---	---	---	56.1	---	---	---	---
	95 YTD		235.7	---	---	---	---	---	235.7	---	---	---	---
	94 YTD		555.7	---	---	---	---	---	555.7	---	---	---	---
WIND IN THE WILLOW BROADWAY PRODUCTION WIND IN THE WILLOWS	Q2	G321	36.3	---	---	---	---	---	36.3	---	---	---	---
	95 YTD		36.3	---	---	---	---	---	36.3	---	---	---	---
WOMEN WARRIOR BROADWAY PRODUCTIONS WOMEN WARRIOR	Q1	G321	73.8	---	---	---	---	---	---	---	---	---	73.8
	95 YTD		73.8	---	---	---	---	---	---	---	---	---	73.8
YM-YWHA 92ND STREET Y CULTURAL EVENTS	Q1	G321	23.7	---	---	23.7	---	---	---	---	---	---	---
	Q2		3.9	---	---	3.9	---	---	---	---	---	---	---
	95 YTD		27.6	---	---	27.6	---	---	---	---	---	---	---
---- CONTINUED ----													

1504

Source 5
LNA Newspaper Spending

Research Company   Leading National Advertisers, Inc. (LNA)

Description   LNA gathers these newspaper space activity reports from publishers of daily newspapers and Sunday magazine supplements. Publishers report on the contracted number of column inches for each firm and/or brand. The cost is calculated from the newspaper's open (no discount) rate. Charges for color, preprints, and the like are added where appropriate.

Function   Source users can learn which newspapers are being used by competitors, and the extent of use as reflected by estimated dollars spent.

Format Notes   The dollar estimates are made in decimal form, and reflect thousands of dollars. Thus, if you saw an estimate as 0.5, you would know that it meant a $500 investment.

Space limits make it necessary for LNA to abbreviate cities and/or the newspaper titles. Those acquainted with using this service would look at ''San Fran Exam Chron'' and translate this to mean the *San Francisco Examiner Chronicle*. After practice the abbreviations seem to disappear.

BUSINESS & FINANCIAL

CLASS/COMPANY/ BRAND/NEWSPAPER	Y-T-D $(000)	JAN $(000)	FEB $(000)	MAR $(000)	1ST QTR $(000)	APR $(000)	MAY ($(000)	JUN $(000)	2ND QTR $(000)
**B111 CONSTRUCTION, ENGINEERING & ARCHIT SRVCS									
company unknown/HERITAGE HOME WORKS CONTRACTOR (CONT'D)									
SAN FRAN EXAM CHRON	5.3	2.1	2.1	0.8	4.9	0.4	---	---	0.4
NEWSPAPERS	25.8	2.2	2.1	0.9	5.1	0.4	17.9	2.5	20.7
company unknown/HOME BUILDERS ASSN OF GREATER CHICAGO									
CHICAGO TRIBUNE	25.1	19.1	---	---	19.1	6.1	---	---	6.1
company unknown/HOME IMPROVEMENT SPECIALISTS									
LA DAILY NEWS	1.2	1.2	---	---	1.2	---	---	---	---
LOS ANGELES TIMES	35.7	---	---	---	---	9.7	13.0	13.0	35.7
NEWSPAPERS	37.0	1.2	---	---	1.2	9.7	13.0	13.0	35.7
company unknown/HOME WINDOW CO CONTRACTORS									
DETROIT NWS FREE PRS	243.4	25.6	25.6	51.3	102.5	51.3	51.3	38.4	140.9
company unknown/IMPERIAL REFINISHING CONTRACTOR									
ALAMEDA TIMES STAR	1.1	0.3	0.2	0.2	0.7	0.2	0.2	---	0.4
ASBURY PARK PRESS	0.9	---	---	---	---	---	0.1	0.7	0.9
BERGEN RECORD	0.8	---	---	---	---	---	0.1	0.7	0.8
BOSTON GLOBE	2.1	1.2	0.9	---	2.1	---	---	---	---
BOSTON HERALD	4.7	1.1	0.9	0.7	2.7	---	0.7	1.3	2.0
CAMDEN COURIER-POST	2.6	---	0.1	0.6	0.7	0.5	0.7	0.7	1.9
CHICAGO TRIBUNE	2.8	---	1.0	1.1	2.0	0.6	0.2	---	0.8
DENVER POST	1.9	---	---	---	---	---	0.9	1.1	1.9
DENVER RCKY MTN NEWS	10.2	2.3	1.6	1.7	5.6	1.9	1.3	1.3	4.5
FREMONT ARGUS	2.6	0.6	0.5	0.5	1.6	0.5	0.5	---	1.0
HAYWARD DAILY REVIEW	4.7	1.1	0.9	0.9	2.9	0.9	0.9	---	1.8
LOS ANGELES TIMES	8.9	1.8	1.4	1.5	4.7	1.3	1.6	1.3	4.2
NEW BRUNSWCK HME NWS	0.4	---	---	---	---	---	0.1	0.3	0.4
NEWARK STAR LEDGER	4.0	1.9	0.8	1.3	4.0	---	---	---	---
OAKLAND TRIBUNE	9.0	2.1	1.7	1.7	5.6	1.7	1.7	---	3.4
PHIL INQUIRER	9.3	1.5	1.3	1.7	4.4	2.0	1.4	1.5	4.8
PLEASANTON VALLY HLD	2.8	0.7	0.5	0.5	1.7	0.5	0.5	---	1.1
SAN FRAN EXAM CHRON	1.4	1.2	0.2	---	1.4	---	---	---	---
SAN JOSE MERCURY-NEW	0.8	0.8	---	---	0.8	---	---	---	---
WASHINGTON POST	12.1	2.4	1.9	1.8	6.2	2.1	2.0	1.8	5.9
WOODBRIDGE NEWS TRIB	0.5	---	---	---	---	---	0.1	0.4	0.5
NEWSPAPERS	83.6	19.2	14.0	14.2	47.3	12.2	13.1	11.0	36.3
company unknown/INTERSPACE DESIGN									
PLEASANTON VALLY HLD	0.2	---	---	0.1	0.1	---	---	0.1	0.1
PLEASANTON VALLY TMS	0.0	---	0.0	---	0.0	---	---	---	---
SAN FRAN CHRONICLE	9.2	---	---	---	---	5.7	2.3	1.2	9.2
SAN FRAN EXAM CHRON	0.3	---	---	0.3	0.3	---	---	---	---
SAN FRAN EXAMINER	1.2	---	---	---	---	1.2	---	---	1.2
SAN JOSE MERCURY-NEW	34.1	11.4	7.6	---	18.9	7.6	---	7.6	15.1
NEWSPAPERS	45.0	11.4	7.6	0.3	19.3	14.5	2.3	8.9	25.7
SUNDAY MAGS	109.3	38.0	8.1	27.4	73.5	16.3	7.8	11.7	35.8
BRAND EXP	154.3	49.3	15.8	27.7	92.8	30.8	10.1	20.6	61.5
company unknown/JOHNNY B QUICK HOME IMPROVEMENT									
WASHINGTON POST	106.9	22.6	17.0	16.9	56.5	16.9	19.4	14.2	50.4
company unknown/KELLY WINDOW & DOOR CONTRACTORS									
ALAMEDA TIMES STAR	2.8	---	0.3	0.8	1.0	0.6	0.8	0.4	1.8
CONTRA COSTA TIMES	0.3	---	---	---	---	0.3	---	---	0.3
FREMONT ARGUS	7.8	---	0.7	2.3	3.0	1.5	1.9	1.3	4.8
HAYWARD DAILY REVIEW	13.3	---	1.3	3.4	4.7	2.8	3.5	2.4	8.6
OAKLAND TRIBUNE	18.6	---	1.9	4.9	6.8	4.1	5.1	2.6	11.8
PLEASANTON VALLY HLD	7.9	---	0.8	2.0	2.8	1.6	2.1	1.4	5.1
PLEASANTON VALLY TMS	0.7	---	---	0.3	0.3	0.4	---	---	0.4
RICHMOND W CTY TMS	0.1	---	---	---	---	0.1	---	---	0.1
NEWSPAPERS	51.4	---	4.9	13.7	18.6	11.4	13.4	8.1	32.8

Source 6
Nielsen National Television Audience Estimates
....

Research Company	Nielsen Media Research
Description	This is the only service that regularly estimates the audiences for national television programs. These estimates are generated by the 4,000+ sample of "people meter" households in the United States. Included in the reporting are the traditional networks (ABC, CBS, FOX, NBC), cable networks (ESPN, USA, etc.), premium cable channels (HBO, Showtime), and others.
Function	Although audience descriptions are limited in this bimonthly "Pocketpiece" NTI, this is the official monitor of program popularity. As such, it is pivotal research in evaluating television advertising investments. It is similarly important for network programming strategies. Contract extensions and cancellations are directly connected to the NTI.
Format Notes	The excerpt shown is for prime evening, but households viewing, household rating, and share of audience figures are constant for measuring all parts of the day, each day of the week.
	"HHLD Audience (000)." This is the estimated count of households viewing each program (as an average of all quarter hours measured). The sample estimates are projected against a universe of 95,400,000 TV homes.
	"HHLD Audience %." This is the home viewing expressed as a percent of all television homes. It is the average household rating for each program regardless of length. As an absolute statistic, the percentage reflects audience size.
	"Share Audience." Called the "popularity indicator," share is based upon the total viewing done in the quarter hour. It is the program's share of the *available* audience. This is a comparative statistic because it does not indicate the actual size of the audience.
	"TA% AVG. AUD.1/2 HR%." The initials TA reflect total audience or the unduplicated percentage of homes exposed during the duration of the program. Notice that the first "TA" figure is always larger than "HHLD Audience %" because the total counts a home even if only one quarter hour was viewed. The subsequent figures on the line are half hour averages for programs of an hour or longer.
Illustration	To demonstrate the NTI format use the program "Northern Exposure" running on CBS from 10:00 to 11:00 p.m.
	The average number of homes viewing (average of four quarter hours) is 8,780,000. This total converts to an average household rating of 9.2. The total percentage of homes viewing at least one quarter hour is 12.2 ("TA%"). The program had an average share of audience of 16 percent (15 percent for the first half-hour, and 16 percent for the second). The average "HHLD Audience" rating for quarter hours is: 9.2, 9.2, 9.0, and 9.2 respectively.

Nielsen NATIONAL TV AUDIENCE ESTIMATES — EVE. WED. FEB. 15,

A-6

TIME	7:00	7:15	7:30	7:45	8:00	8:15	8:30	8:45	9:00	9:15	9:30	9:45	10:00	10:15	10:30	10:45
HUT	58.4	59.6	60.9	62.5	64.6	66.2	66.8	67.3	66.0	65.8	64.8	64.2	61.3	59.7	57.6	55.0

ABC TV (→ PRIMETIME LIVE → ; → NORTHERN EXPOSURE →)

Programs: SISTER, SISTER · ALL AMERICAN GIRL · ROSEANNE · ELLEN (PAE) · PRIMETIME LIVE

Program	HHLD% & (000)	74% AVG. AUD. 1/2 HR %	SHARE %	AVG. AUD. BY 1/4 HR %
SISTER, SISTER	9.7 / 9,250	12.3	15	9.4
ALL AMERICAN GIRL	10.1 / 9,640	11.5	15	9.6 / 10.6
ROSEANNE	15.5 / 14,790	18.4	24	14.9 / 16.2
ELLEN (PAE)	14.7 / 14,020	17.2	23	14.7 / 14.1
PRIMETIME LIVE	13.3 / 12,690	19.6 / 14.1*	23 / 22*	14.1 / 14.2 / 13.0 / 12.1 / 12.5*

CBS TV

Programs: DISNEY'S NANCY KERRIGAN DREAMS ON ICE · NANNY-WED (R) · DAVE'S WORLD-WED (R) · NORTHERN EXPOSURE

Program	HHLD% & (000)	74% AVG. AUD. 1/2 HR %	SHARE %	AVG. AUD. BY 1/4 HR %
DISNEY'S NANCY KERRIGAN DREAMS ON ICE	10.0 / 9,540	9.8* / 10.1*	15* / 15*	9.6 / 10.3 / 9.9
NANNY-WED (R)	9.2 / 8,780	11.2	14	9.0
DAVE'S WORLD-WED (R)	7.8 / 7,440	9.4	12	7.8 / 7.9
NORTHERN EXPOSURE	9.2 / 8,780	12.2 / 9.1*	16 / 16*	9.2 / 9.0 / 9.2

NBC TV

Programs: WHEN STARS WERE KIDS · DATELINE NBC-WED · LAW AND ORDER

Program	HHLD% & (000)	74% AVG. AUD. 1/2 HR %	SHARE %	AVG. AUD. BY 1/4 HR %
WHEN STARS WERE KIDS	10.5 / 10,020	15.8 / 10.1*	16 / 15*	9.8 / 10.4 / 10.8
DATELINE NBC-WED	11.2 / 10,680	17.7 / 10.9* / 12.0*	17 / 16* / 19*	10.9 / 11.0 / 11.7
LAW AND ORDER	12.6 / 12,020	15.8 / 12.3* / 12.9*	22 / 20* / 23*	12.2 / 12.4 / 12.8 / 12.9

FOX TV

Programs: BEVERLY HILLS, 90210 (PAE) · PARTY OF FIVE

Program	HHLD% & (000)	74% AVG. AUD. 1/2 HR %	SHARE %	AVG. AUD. BY 1/4 HR %
BEVERLY HILLS, 90210 (PAE)	11.2 / 10,680	14.3 / 10.9* / 11.5*	17 / 17* / 17*	10.6 / 11.2 / 11.4 / 11.6
PARTY OF FIVE	6.5 / 6,200	9.7 / 6.6* / 6.3*	10 / 10* / 10*	7.0 / 6.3 / 6.2

INDEPENDENTS (INCLUDING SUPERSTATIONS EXCEPT TBS)

	7:15	7:45	8:00	8:30	8:45	9:00	9:30	9:45	10:00	10:45
AVERAGE AUDIENCE	16.5 (+F)	17.3 (+F)	8.7	8.7	9.0	8.9	8.7	8.7	12.6 (+F)	10.8 (+F)
SHARE AUDIENCE %	28	28	13	13	13	14	13	13	21	19

PBS

	7:15	7:45	8:00	8:30	8:45	9:00	9:30	9:45	10:00	10:45
AVERAGE AUDIENCE	1.2	1.6	3.1	3.2	3.6	1.9	1.6	1.6	1.5	1.1
SHARE AUDIENCE %	2	3	5	5	5	3	2	3	2	2

CABLE ORIG. (INCLUDING TBS)

	7:15	7:45	8:00	8:30	8:45	9:00	9:30	10:00	10:45
AVERAGE AUDIENCE	14.6 (+F)	15.3 (+F)	16.9	17.8	17.8	17.6	18.0	15.4 (+F)	13.9 (+F)
SHARE AUDIENCE %	25	25	26	27	27	27	28	25	25

PAY SERVICES

	7:15	7:45	8:00	8:30	8:45	9:00	9:30	10:00	10:45
AVERAGE AUDIENCE	1.5	1.6	3.2	3.6	3.6	3.6	3.3	3.8	3.6
SHARE AUDIENCE %	3	3	5	5	6	6	5	6	6

U.S. TV Households: 95,400,000

A-7   For SPANISH LANGUAGE TELEVISION audience estimates, see the Nielsen Hispanic Television Index (NHTI) TV Audience Report.

For explanation of symbols. See page B

Source 7
Nielsen Station Index (NSI) Audience Estimates for Local Market Television
....

Research Company   Nielsen Media Research

Description   Every television market in the Continental United States receives periodic measurement for station and program popularity. The largest markets are reported monthly, and the smallest are measured three times per year ("sweeps"). These reports, known as "Nielsen Station Index (NSI) Reports," are generated from a combination of electronic metered and diary-reported households. The reports estimate audiences by household, gender, and age. Measures are offered for two geographic areas: the metropolitan area, and a larger area known as the "designated market area" or "DMA."

Function   These reports are designed to assist buyers and sellers of television advertising in estimating the size and composition of local audiences for all dayparts and types of programs.

Format Notes   The NSI report has a complex format intended to provide current and past history for the programs or stations listed. To assist your interpretation of the data, some of the most important elements are explained.

"DMA Household and Persons Ratings."   As noted above, the DMA is an area determined by television boundaries. It is a predetermined list of counties assigned to a home TV market. The assignment by Nielsen is based on combined popularity of a home market's commercial stations. Each county showing a preponderance of viewing is assigned to one home market or another. Ratings are percentages based on all possible viewing homes or people whether they were viewing or not.

"HUT/PUT Totals."   These are the summed ratings for all stations during the time period. The letters HUT mean "homes using television;" PUT means "people viewing television." Both figures are necessary to calculate shares of audience. Recall that share is not calculated on possible viewing audience (rating), but on those actually using television at the time.

"Share Trend."   The figures cover the three preceding reports for this market. This share history helps buyers judge the consistency of station popularity in case programming should change in the future.

Illustration   Follow one program to see how the NSI works. The example is KDAF's "Saturday Movie" from 1:30 to 2:00. The "metro" and "DMA" Household Ratings (Multi-Week AVG)" are both 8.0, indicating consistent coverage. Averages can be misleading, especially for programs that change content as movies do. Not surprising, the movie program did vary in audience from week to week (a low of 6.0 to a high of 10.0).

As you look across the "persons" and "women" and "men" ratings you will notice little number variance. This might suggest that the station programs family-type movies that appeal to men and women of most age segments.

DALLAS-FT. WORTH, TX

WK1 2/02-2/08 WK2 2/09-2/15 WK3 2/16-2/22 WK4 2/23-3/01

SATURDAY 1:00PM - 2:30PM

Column key (left to right): METRO HH [RTG / SHR] · STATION/PROGRAM · DMA HOUSEHOLD RATINGS WEEKS [W1 / W2 / W3 / W4] · MULTI-WEEK AVG [RTG / SHR] · SHARE TREND [NOV94 / MAY94 / FEB94] · DMA RATINGS PERSONS [2+ / 18+ / 12-24 / 12-34 / 18-34 / 18-49 / 21-49 / 25-54 / 35+ / 35-64 / 50+] · WOMEN [18+ / 12-24 / 18-34 / 18-49 / 25-49 / 25-54 / WKG] · MEN [18+ / 18-34 / 18-49 / 21-49 / 25-49 / 25-54] · TNS 12-17 · CHILD [2-11 / 6-11]

R.S.E. THRESHOLDS

RTG 25+% (1 S.E.)	3 3 3 3 / 2 LT	4 WK AVG 50+%	1 1 1 1	
PERSONS 25+%	1 2 6 3 3 2 2 2 2 2 2	WOMEN	2 9 6 3 3 3 3	MEN 2 7 3 3 3 3 / 12-17 9 / CHILD 7 10
PERSONS 50+%	LT LT 1 1 1 1 1 1 LT LT 1 1	WOMEN	LT 2 2 1 1 1 1	MEN 1 2 1 1 1 1 / 12-17 2 / CHILD 2 3

1:00PM

RTG	SHR	STATION	PROGRAM	W1	W2	W3	W4	AVG-R	AVG-S	NOV	MAY	FEB	PERSONS	WOMEN	MEN	12-17	2-11	6-11
7	16	KDAF	SATURDAY MOV	6	7	5	8	7	15	12X	15	13	4 4 6 6 4 5 4 5 3 4 1	4 4 5 5 6 5 5	3 3 4 4 4 4	12	3	4
2	5	KDFI	AVG. ALL WKS	2	3	2	1	2	5	5				1 1 1			
2	5		SAINT	2	3	2			5					1 1 1 1			
1	3		SAT MOV				1	1	3								
3	7	KDFW	AVG. ALL WKS	2	4	4	3	3	6	5	7	18	3 3 5 4 4 4 3 3 2 3 2	2 2 3 3 3 3 4	4 5 7 6 2 2	5		
2	6		CBS NCAA-SAT 1				3	3	6				4 4 10 6 5 5 3 3 2 3 1	2 2 7 4 3 4 4 5	5 7 6 2 2 2	11		
4	8		EYE-SPORTS-SAT		4			4	8				2 3 2 3 4 4 3 3 2 3	3 2 4 5 4 5	5 3 4 4 4 4			
3	8		TWIN 125'S			4		4	9				2 2 2 3 2 2 2 2 4 1	1	3 6 3 3 4 4			
<<	7	KDTN	AMRCN ADVENTRE	<<	<<	<<	1	<<		X			1 2	3 2	1 1		
3	7	KERA	FURNITURE-MEND	2	4	3	2	3	6	5	6	4	1 2 1 1 1 1 2 2 2	3 2 3 2 2 1	1 1 1 1 1			
3	8	KTVT	SWC BKBL	4	5	3	2	3	8	10	9	5	2 2 3 2 2 2 1 2 2 2 4	1 2 1 1 1 1	4 4 3 2 3 3	3		
4	10	KTXA	MOVIE TRAILER	4	5	5	6	4	10	13	10	8	3 3 3 3 4 3 3 3 2 2 1	3 4 6 5 4 4 3 1	2 2 2 2 2 2	1	6	6
1	3	KUVN	ONDA MAX SA	2	1	1	1	1	3	1X	NR	NR	1 1 1 1 1	1 1			2	3
2	4	KXAS	AVG. ALL WKS	1	2	1	2	2	4	7	12	6	1 1 1 1 2 1	1				
1	3		PAID PROGRAM	1												
2	5		FACES-COURAGE		2			2	5				1 1 2 3 5 2	1	1		
1	2		NBC SPORTS-SPC			1		1	2				1 1 1 2 1	1 1 1			
2	5		SPORTSWRLD-SAT				2	2	6				1 1 2 1 3	1	1		
3	7	KXTX	LONE RANGER-SA	3	4	4	2	3	7	7X	9	8	1 1 1 2 2 2 2 1	1 2 2 2 1	1 1 1 2 2	2	3
4	9	WFAA	AVG. ALL WKS	3	3	3	4	3	8	14	8	9	1 1 1 1 1 1 1 1	1 3 2 2 1 1	1 1 1 1	1	
4	9		QUEST	3				3	8				1	2	2 3 2 3		
3	8		WINTER SPRTCST		3	3		3	7				1 3 1 2 1 1	1 5 3 2	1		
4	11		KING-MOUNTAIN				4	4	11				1 1 1 1 1 1	1 3 1 2 2	1	4	
43			HUT/PUT/TOTALS*	40	48	41	40	42		41	37	40	22 22 23 23 22 22 21 21 21 21 21	23 23 26 25 27 24 23	20 19 19 17 18 18	27	18	20

1:30PM

RTG	SHR	STATION	PROGRAM	W1	W2	W3	W4	AVG-R	AVG-S	NOV	MAY	FEB	PERSONS	WOMEN	MEN	12-17	2-11	6-11
8	18	KDAF	SATURDAY MOV	7	8	6	10	8	18	14X	13	13	5 5 8 8 6 6 6 6 6 4 1	5 5 7 6 8 7 5	5 5 6 6 6 5	13	3	4
2	4	KDFI	AVG. ALL WKS	2	3	2	1	2	4	4	7	6		1 1			
2	5		SAINT	2	3	2			5					1 1 1 1			
1	2		SAT MOV				1	1	2								
3	7	KDFW	AVG. ALL WKS	3	3	3	3	3	6	5	5	18	3 3 5 4 4 4 3 3 2 3 1	2 3 3 3 3 3 4	4 6 5 3 3 3	5		
2	5		CBS NCAA-SAT 1	3			3	3	6				4 4 10 7 5 5 3 3 2 3 1	2 7 4 3 4 4 5	5 7 6 2 2 2	11		
3	7		EYE-SPORTS-SAT		3			3	7				2 3 2 3 3 3 3 3 1	2 3 4 4	5 3 4 4 3 3			
3	9		TWIN 125'S			3		3	9				2 2 3 3 2 2 2 1	1	3 6 4 4 4 4			
<<		KDTN	AMRCN ADVENTRE	<<	<<	1	<<	<<		1X							
3	6	KERA	VICTORY GARDEN	2	3	3	2	2	6	4X	6	5	1 2 1 1 1 2 1 1 2 2 3	3 3 2 2 2 1	1 1 1 1			
3	8	KTVT	SWC BKBL	4	4	2	3	4	8	8	11	5	2 2 2 2 1 1 1 1 3 2 5	1 2 1 1 1 1	3 3 2 2 2 2	2		
5	11	KTXA	MOVIE TRAILER	5	5	6	5	5	10	13	9	9	2 2 3 3 4 3 3 2 2 1	3 5 6 4 4 3 2 1	2 2 2 1 1	2	4
1	3	KUVN	ONDA MAX SA	1	1	2	1	1	3	2X	NR	NR	1 1	1 1	1		4	4
2	5	KXAS	AVG. ALL WKS	1	3	2	3	2	7	7	13	6	1 1 1 2 2 3 1	1	1 1 1			
1	3		FOUNDATN-LEGCY	1													
3	7		NBC SPORTS-SPL		3			3	6				2 3 4 5 8 2	2	3 1 1 1 1		
2	4		NBC SPORT-SPCL			2		2	4				1 1 1 1 1 1	1	1 1 1 1		
3	7		SPORTSWRLD-SAT				3	3	7				1 1 1 2 2 3	2	1 1 1 1 1	1	
4	9	KXTX	LONE RNGR SA B	4	5	4	4	4	9	8X	7	8	2 2 2 2 1 2 2 2 2	1 3 2 1	2 1 2 2 2 2	2 3	3
3	8	WFAA	AVG. ALL WKS	3	3	3	4	3	9	15	9	8	1 1 1 1	1 1	1	1	
3	7		QUEST	3				3	7								
3	7		TRAVEL TRAVEL		3	3		3	7				2 2 2 2 1				
4	10		KING-MOUNTAIN				4	4	10				1 1 1 1 1	2	3	3	
43			HUT/PUT/TOTALS*	42	49	40	42	43		42	39	42	22 23 25 25 24 23 22 21 22 21 23	23 23 26 24 27 25 21	22 21 21 19 19 18	30	15	18

2:00PM

RTG	SHR	STATION	PROGRAM	W1	W2	W3	W4	AVG-R	AVG-S	NOV	MAY	FEB	PERSONS	WOMEN	MEN	12-17	2-11	6-11
9	20	KDAF	SATURDAY MOV	9	6	7	12	8	20	15X	9	10	5 5 7 7 6 7 6 7 6 4 1	5 4 7 7 8 7 6	4 5 6 6 6 5	11	4	5
2	5	KDFI	AVG. ALL WKS	3	2	2	1	2	4	5	7	8	1 1 1 1 1 1 1 1 1 1 1	1 1 1 1 1 1	1 1 2 2 2 1			
3	8		SWC BKBL	3	2	2			5				1 1 1 1 1 1 1 1	1 1 1 1	1 2 2 1		
1	2		SAT MOV				1	1	2								
3	8	KDFW	AVG. ALL WKS	3	6	2	3	3	9	4	6	18	2 2 1 1 3 2 3 2 3 1 6	2 1 3 3 3	3 3 3 3 1			
2	6		PEBBLE BCH-SA	3				3	7				2 2 1 1 1 2 1 3 1 6	1 1 1 2	3 3 3 1			
6	11		EYE-SPORTS-SAT		6			6	12				4 5 4 6 6 7 4 4 2	5 6 8 8 7	5 7 6 6 7 6			
1	6		TWIN 125'S			2		2	6				1 1 1 1 2 1 1	1	2 4 2 3 2			
3	8		NISSAN-OPEN SA				3	3	8				2 3 4 3 3 2 1 1 5 2	2 2 2 2 4	4 3 1 1 1 3	3		
<<		KDTN	PRNCP-ACCNTNG	<<	<<	<<	<<	<<		X							
3	8	KERA	HOMETIME	3	4	4	3	3	7	5X	8	6	1 2 1 1 2 2 2 2 2 2 2	2 2 2 2	1 2 2 2	2		1
3	8	KTVT	AVG. ALL WKS	4	4	4	4	4	8	8	11	5	2 2 2 2 3 3 2 2 3 3 1	3 5 3 3 3 3	2 3 3 4 4 3	3		
4	8		SAT SHOWCASE 2	4	4			3	8				2 3 2 3 2 3 3 3 1	2 3 3 3 3	2 3 4 4 3		1	2
3	7		SWC BKBL			3	4	2	8				1 1 3 2 2 1 2 1	1 1 1	1 2 2 2			
4	10	KTXA	SAT MOVIE 2	4	6	2	4	4	10	10X	9	5	2 3 1 2 2 2 2 2 2 3	2 2 3 4 3 4	1 1 1	2	6	10
1	2	KUVN	DE PELICULA SA	1	1	<<	1	1	2	2	NR	NR	1 1 1 1 1 1 1	1 1 1	1 2 1	1	
2	5	KXAS	AVG. ALL WKS	1	4	3	3	2	6	7	13	7	1 2 1 1 2 3 2	1 1 1	2 3 3 3			
1	3		FOUNDATN-LEGCY	1													
4	8		NBC SPORTS-SPL		4			4	7				2 3 1 2 5 6 7 2	2	3 3 3		
2	6		NBC SPORT-SPCL			3		3	7				1 1 1 1 1 1	1	1 1 1		
2	5		NBC SPRTS SPCL				3	3	7				2 2 4 4 4 5 4	3 4 3 4	4 4 5 4		
4	10	KXTX	RIFLEMAN	3	6	4	4	4	10	8X	8	9	2 3 1 2 2 3 3 2 3	2 2 3 3	3 4 4 5 4	1	1	2
4	8	WFAA	PRO BOWLR TOUR	4	4	3	4	4	9	18	10	8	2 2 1 1 1 2 2 3 2 4 2	2 1 1 2 3 2	2 2 2 2 2			
43			HUT/PUT/TOTALS*	43	48	40	41	43		43	39	42	23 25 20 22 21 24 25 25 27 26 26	25 18 23 24 27 26 24	25 19 24 25 25 24	24	17	22

SATURDAY 1:00PM - 2:30PM

FEBRUARY

Source 8
Arbitron Radio Local Market Reports
....

Research Company   Arbitron

Description   Each market's rating data are collected from personal, one-week diaries completed by each household member above the age of twelve. Sample sizes are statistically derived and vary by market.

The emphasis in these reports is to measure each station's listeners per 15 minutes ("quarter-hour") throughout the day. Listeners are estimated in two ways: 1) average number in the audience for each quarter-hour segment, and 2) cumulative listeners, or how many different people will listen to at least one quarter-hour sometime during the week.

Function   The reports are set up to estimate audiences by age segment and by gender. Advertising and marketing firms use these to gauge the popularity of a station(s) in delivering desired target audiences. Stations and dayparts are chosen, in part, from these rating reports.

Format Notes   The excerpt shown on the next page is from a San Francisco market report. The audience reported is confined to women between the ages of 25 and 49.

Two geographic areas are reported. The *total survey area* ("TSA") reports listenership from the metropolitan area and many other surrounding counties. Because radio stations vary significantly in distance coverage, marketers are often interested in all the listeners regardless of residence location. The *metro* estimates are confined to the area defined by the federal government's "Metropolitan Statistical Area." These estimates appeal to companies selling products or services concentrated close to the city and suburbs.

"AQH" (average quarter hour).   AQH is the estimated number of listeners (e.g., headcount) during a 15-minute segment. Note: you only have to report 5 minutes of listening to be credited.

"Cume" (cumulative listening).   Cume is the estimated number of *different* listeners within a reported part of the day (e.g., during all quarter hours from 6 to 10 a.m. Monday thru Friday).

"AQH" Rating.   The AQH Rating is estimated listenership expressed as a percentage of the audience segment. Thus, a 1.0 rating means one percent of women 25 to 49 in the area were part of a station's audience.

"AQH" Share.   The AQH Share is also a percentage reflecting the proportion of total listeners listening to a particular station. Thus, a 10 percent share for a station would mean its proportion of all who were listening. It does not reflect the audience size (1 of 10 and 1,000 of 10,000 are both 10 percent shares).

Illustration   Assume your firm is interested in this target audience, with particular emphasis on full-time employment. For this reason you are most interested in the morning commuting audience (6 to 10 a.m.) and in the total survey area.

Which is the top station? By most measures it is KBLX AM and FM combined (simulcast radio). Arbitron estimates that an average quarter hour will find 17,500 women between 25 and 49 in the audience. The station's share is also highest at 5.6 percent of the metro area.

If you are interested in reaching the largest unduplicated (cume) audience you might consider KCBS. It is estimated to cover 110,900 different women within the daypart on a five-day basis.

Target Audience
WOMEN 25-49

Target Audience - Women

	MONDAY-FRIDAY 6AM-10AM				MONDAY-FRIDAY 10AM-3PM				MONDAY-FRIDAY 3PM-7PM				MONDAY-FRIDAY 7PM-MID				WEEKEND 10AM-7PM			
	AQH (00)	CUME (00)	AQH RTG	AQH SHR	AQH (00)	CUME (00)	AQH RTG	AQH SHR	AQH (00)	CUME (00)	AQH RTG	AQH SHR	AQH (00)	CUME (00)	AQH RTG	AQH SHR	AQH (00)	CUME (00)	AQH RTG	AQH SHR
KABL																				
METRO	14	93	.1	.4	5	78		.2	7	118	.1	.3	5	77		.6	10	88	.1	.5
TSA	14	93			5	78			7	118			5	77			12	93		
KABL-FM																				
METRO	60	636	.5	1.9	65	549	.5	2.1	59	676	.4	2.3	29	380	.2	3.2	40	316	.3	1.9
TSA	61	648			67	555			61	682			29	380			41	332		
KARA																				
METRO	37	259	.3	1.2	79	277	.6	2.5	53	329	.4	2.0	10	109	.1	1.1	29	181	.2	1.4
TSA	38	279			80	295			55	347			11	128			29	185		
KBAY																				
METRO	24	226	.2	.8	22	162	.2	.7	20	190	.2	.8	13	143	.1	1.4	26	155	.2	1.3
TSA	38	306			39	224			31	237			13	151			30	192		
KBLX																				
METRO	21	67	.2	.7	22	111	.2	.7	12	62	.1	.5	11	103	.1	1.2	13	69	.1	.6
TSA	21	67			22	119			13	70			11	103			13	69		
KBLX-FM																				
METRO	154	934	1.2	4.9	183	948	1.4	5.8	141	1008	1.1	5.4	39	559	.3	4.3	127	845	1.0	6.1
TSA	154	940			184	954			141	1014			40	574			127	851		
A/F TOT																				
METRO	175	988	1.3	5.6	205	1010	1.5	6.5	153	1045	1.2	5.9	50	617	.4	5.6	140	875	1.1	6.8
TSA	175	994			206	1024			154	1059			51	632			140	881		
KBRG																				
METRO	27	142	.2	.9	24	144	.2	.8	21	176	.2	.8	13	79	.1	1.4	21	142	.2	1.0
TSA	27	142			24	144			21	185			13	94			21	142		
KCBS																				
METRO	110	976	.8	3.5	43	617	.3	1.4	70	831	.5	2.7	17	440	.1	1.9	29	395	.2	1.4
TSA	132	1109			57	723			75	920			18	456			45	464		
KDFC																				
METRO						28														
TSA						28														
KDFC-FM																				
METRO	24	382	.2	.8	27	432	.2	.9	32	450	.2	1.2	24	387	.2	2.7	24	282	.2	1.2
TSA	29	400			27	441			32	450			24	387			29	314		
A/F TOT																				
METRO	24	382	.2	.8	27	442	.2	.9	32	450	.2	1.2	24	387	.2	2.7	24	282	.2	1.2
TSA	29	400			27	451			32	450			24	387			29	314		
KDIA																				
METRO	67	256	.5	2.1	54	230	.4	1.7	27	183	.2	1.0	24	136	.2	2.7	52	254	.4	2.5
TSA	67	256			54	230			27	183			24	136			52	254		
KEZR																				
METRO	53	373	.4	1.7	79	342	.6	2.5	72	431	.5	2.8	15	193	.1	1.7	33	297	.2	1.6
TSA	53	383			80	346			72	445			15	197			33	297		
KFAX																				
METRO	39	238	.3	1.2	35	145	.3	1.1	45	205	.3	1.7	20	88	.2	2.2	23	126	.2	1.1
TSA	39	238			35	145			45	205			20	88			23	126		
KFOG																				
METRO	76	670	.6	2.4	79	589	.6	2.5	77	719	.6	3.0	46	472	.3	5.1	73	499	.5	3.5
TSA	78	686			79	604			78	734			46	482			74	517		
KFRC																				
METRO	38	218	.3	1.2	53	234	.4	1.7	30	258	.2	1.2	4	123		.4	8	56	.1	.4
TSA	40	237			54	243			32	268			5	135			11	70		
KFRC-FM																				
METRO	84	654	.6	2.7	88	563	.7	2.8	69	748	.5	2.7	14	244	.1	1.6	33	406	.2	1.6
TSA	84	677			89	586			69	748			14	244			37	450		
KGO																				
METRO	164	1041	1.2	5.3	117	766	.9	3.7	106	870	.8	4.1	40	399	.3	4.4	69	551	.5	3.3
TSA	187	1213			141	922			133	1025			51	496			76	623		
KHQT																				
METRO	30	219	.2	1.0	27	229	.2	.9	21	326	.2	.8	4	98		.4	12	196	.1	.6
TSA	30	219			27	229			21	332			4	98			12	196		
KIOI																				
METRO	240	1338	1.8	7.7	241	1095	1.8	7.6	135	1028	1.0	5.2	27	539	.2	3.0	96	894	.7	4.6
TSA	241	1348			242	1110			136	1068			27	556			97	916		
KIQI																				
METRO	23	126	.2	.7	34	116	.3	1.1	8	130	.1	.3	5	63		.6	20	119	.2	1.0
TSA	23	132			34	116			8	136			5	69			20	119		
KITS																				
METRO	109	667	.8	3.5	131	724	1.0	4.1	80	712	.6	3.1	26	440	.2	2.9	73	605	.5	3.5
TSA	114	726			132	733			86	745			28	469			75	634		
KJAZ																				
METRO	2	67		.1	11	155	.1	.3	19	209	.1	.7	21	223	.2	2.3	11	152	.1	.5
TSA	2	67			11	155			19	209			21	223			11	156		
KKHI																				
METRO	1	30			10	30	.1	.3	9	30	.1	.3	2	16		.2	1	15		
TSA	1	30			10	30			9	30			2	16			1	15		
KKHI-FM																				
METRO	16	190	.1	.5	16	215	.1	.5	16	199	.1	.6	9	164	.1	1.0	10	154	.1	.5
TSA	16	195			17	248			18	209			11	183			13	167		
A/F TOT																				
METRO	17	221	.1	.5	26	230	.2	.8	25	213	.2	1.0	11	179	.1	1.2	11	169	.1	.5
TSA	17	226			27	262			27	224			13	198			14	182		
KKIQ																				
METRO	27	155	.2	.9	22	100	.2	.7	17	146	.1	.7	6	74		.7	9	136	.1	.4
TSA	36	167			35	124			27	179			6	74			10	150		

Footnote Symbols: * Audience estimates adjusted for actual broadcast schedule. + Station(s) changed call letters since the prior survey - see Page 5B.

ARBITRON

Source 9
SMRB Demographic Status of Adult Magazine Readers
••

Research Company   Simmons Market Research Bureau, Inc. (SMRB)

Description   This is part of an annual report by SMRB (1991 example) using data and information compiled from personal interviews with over 23,000 adults.

Each magazine's readership is determined from a face-to-face interview using a "recent reading" methodology that is recall based. The initial interview is followed in 6 to 8 weeks by another to expand readership habits and frequencies.

Function   This portion of the report is used to establish the very basic demographics of the gender of readership (the number and percentage of male vs. female readers). In addition, our excerpt covers a role called "principal shoppers." This reflects readership of magazines by the primary "purchasing agent" for each household unit.

Although this information is of reasonable interest to all marketers, it is of particular interest to those whose products or services are heavily dependent on either males or females. Unwanted readers are reflected in the price of an advertising page.

Format Notes   To use this format, which is also employed by a competing service (MRI), each of the columns must be understood. Each contributes a different perspective on the magazine.

"Total U.S."   This data column on the far left side shows the total estimated readers for each publication—regardless of any segment or category. It is the total average issue readers.

Column "A."   This is the projected *number* of readers per average issue. "A" counts the number of adult, or male, or female, or principal shopper readers for each publication.

Column "B."   This is the representative percentage of the "A" column. If you saw a 10.0 under the "Adults" B column, you would know that 10 percent of U.S. adults read an average issue of that publication. To verify, divide any column A number by the number at the very top of "A." The figure you have is shown in "B."

Column "C."   This column has a different reference than columns "A" and B." They were based on the demographic or target segment (i.e., "Males"). Column "C" is calculated on the total readers of the magazine. The column number answers this question: what percentage of magazine X's readership fits in each of the heading categories? If you saw a 10.0 under the males category, it would mean that 10 percent of the magazine's readership is male. To verify, divide any column A number by the total readership number (under "Total U.S."). The figure you have is shown in "C."

Column "D."   This column shows an index ("INDX"). It compares two percentages; the one for each publication in column "C" and the one at the very top of the "C" column. The top percentage is the U.S. figure. For example, the top percentage under the "female" heading in column "C" is 52.3. Of all U.S. adults, 52.3 are female. To create the index found in column "D" this figure is divided *into* the percentage for each publication listed under column "C."

Indices are quick indicators of relationship. For example, an index of 130 is an above-average relationship. A 70 index is below average. A magazine with a 130 index under "females" would tell you that you are more likely to find a female reader in this publication than you would from the total U.S. population.

Illustration On the excerpt find *People* magazine. Here is what the columns mean for *People* using the female category.

"**Total U.S.**" The average issue of *People* is read by 28,488,000 adults.

"**Column A.**" The average issue is read by 18,756,000 females.

"**Column B.**" 19.7 percent of U.S. adult females read the average issue of *People*.

"**Column C.**" 65.8 percent of all readers of *People* are female.

"**Column D.**" The 126 means you are more likely (26 points above average) to find a female reader in *People* magazines's readership than you would from sampling the U.S. adult population.

```
0007                              DEMOGRAPHIC STATUS                                    0007
M-1                                   (ADULTS)                                          M-1
```

	TOTAL U.S. '000	ADULTS A '000	B % DOWN	C ACROSS %	D INDX	MALES A '000	B % DOWN	C ACROSS %	D INDX	FEMALES A '000	B % DOWN	C ACROSS %	D INDX	PRINCIPAL SHOPPERS A '000	B % DOWN	C ACROSS %	D INDX
TOTAL	182456	182456	100.0	100.0	100	87118	100.0	47.7	100	95338	100.0	52.3	100	105724	100.0	57.9	100
THE NEW YORKER	2576	2576	1.4	100.0	100	1205	1.4	46.8	98	1371	1.4	53.2	102	1491	1.4	57.9	100
NEWSWEEK	21396	21396	11.7	100.0	100	12746	14.6	59.6	125	8650	9.1	40.4	77	11018	10.4	51.5	89
THE N.Y. TIMES MAGAZINE	3859	3859	2.1	100.0	100	2221	2.5	57.6	121	1637	1.7	42.4	81	1960	1.9	50.8	88
OMNI	2338	2338	1.3	100.0	100	1635	1.9	69.9	146	703	0.7	30.1	58	1089	1.0	46.6	80
1,001 HOME IDEAS	3771	3771	2.1	100.0	100	995	1.1	26.4	55	2777	2.9	73.6	141	2810	2.7	74.5	129
ORGANIC GARDENING	2544	2544	1.4	100.0	100	1004	1.2	39.5	83	1540	1.6	60.5	116	1712	1.6	67.3	116
OUTDOOR LIFE	7310	7310	4.0	100.0	100	5765	6.6	78.9	165	1545	1.6	21.1	40	2959	2.8	40.5	70
PARADE MAGAZINE	67853	67853	37.2	100.0	100	32878	37.7	48.5	101	34975	36.7	51.5	99	38699	36.6	57.0	98
PARENTING	1947	1947	1.1	100.0	100	312	0.4	16.0	34	1635	1.7	84.0	161	1442	1.4	74.1	128
PARENTS	6643	6643	3.6	100.0	100	1149	1.3	17.3	36	5495	5.8	82.7	158	4809	4.5	72.4	125
PEOPLE	28488	28488	15.6	100.0	100	9732	11.2	34.2	72	18756	19.7	65.8	126	18009	17.0	63.2	109
PLAYBOY	8337	8337	4.6	100.0	100	7306	8.4	87.6	184	1031	1.1	12.4	24	3316	3.1	39.8	69
POPULAR MECHANICS	5655	5655	3.1	100.0	100	5067	5.8	89.6	188	588	0.6	10.4	20	2015	1.9	35.6	61
POPULAR SCIENCE	4555	4555	2.5	100.0	100	3811	4.4	83.7	175	745	0.8	16.4	31	1857	1.8	40.8	70
PRACTICAL HOMEOWNER	1281	1281	0.7	100.0	100	705	0.8	55.0	115	577	0.6	45.0	86	590	0.6	46.1	79
PREVENTION	6154	6154	3.4	100.0	100	1551	1.8	25.2	53	4603	4.8	74.8	143	4440	4.2	72.1	125
READER'S DIGEST	36930	36930	20.2	100.0	100	15022	17.2	40.7	85	21909	23.0	59.3	114	22703	21.5	61.5	106
REDBOOK	10533	10533	5.8	100.0	100	971	1.1	9.2	19	9563	10.0	90.8	174	8467	8.0	80.4	139
ROAD & TRACK	3838	3838	2.1	100.0	100	3563	4.1	92.8	194	275	0.3	7.2	14	1171	1.1	30.5	53
ROLLING STONE	6154	6154	3.4	100.0	100	3806	4.4	61.8	130	2348	2.5	38.2	73	2825	2.7	45.9	79
SCIENTIFIC AMERICAN	1835	1835	1.0	100.0	100	1302	1.5	71.0	149	533	0.6	29.0	56	943	0.9	51.4	89
SELF	2957	2957	1.6	100.0	100	*135	0.2	4.6	10	2822	3.0	95.4	183	2193	2.1	74.2	128
SESAME STREET MAGAZINE	3606	3606	2.0	100.0	100	764	0.9	21.2	44	2843	3.0	78.8	151	2657	2.5	73.7	127
SEVENTEEN	3532	3532	1.9	100.0	100	319	0.4	9.0	19	3213	3.4	91.0	174	2135	2.0	60.4	104
SHAPE	1664	1664	0.9	100.0	100	248	0.3	14.9	31	1416	1.5	85.1	163	1206	1.1	72.5	125
SKI	1764	1764	1.0	100.0	100	1228	1.4	69.6	146	536	0.6	30.4	58	874	0.8	49.5	86
SKIING	1535	1535	0.8	100.0	100	1032	1.2	67.2	141	502	0.5	32.7	63	842	0.8	54.9	95
SMITHSONIAN	6299	6299	3.5	100.0	100	3311	3.8	52.6	110	2987	3.1	47.4	91	3505	3.3	55.6	96
SOAP OPERA DIGEST	6437	6437	3.5	100.0	100	404	0.5	6.3	13	6034	6.3	93.7	179	4628	4.4	71.9	124
SOUTHERN LIVING	7213	7213	4.0	100.0	100	1998	2.3	27.7	58	5216	5.5	72.3	138	4795	4.5	66.5	115
SPORT	3012	3012	1.7	100.0	100	2679	3.1	88.9	186	333	0.3	11.1	21	1171	1.1	38.9	67
THE SPORTING NEWS	3348	3348	1.8	100.0	100	2904	3.3	86.7	182	445	0.5	13.3	25	1357	1.3	40.5	70
SPORTS AFIELD	3370	3370	1.8	100.0	100	2754	3.2	81.7	171	616	0.6	18.3	35	1415	1.3	42.0	72
SPORTS ILLUSTRATED	21035	21035	11.5	100.0	100	17260	19.8	82.1	172	3775	4.0	17.9	34	8372	7.9	39.8	69
STAR	10704	10704	5.9	100.0	100	3085	3.5	28.8	60	7619	8.0	71.2	136	7147	6.8	66.8	115

Source 10
Circulation '95 (Newspaper Circulation Analysis by DMA Area)
....

Research Company Standard Rate and Data Service (SRDS)

Description This annual service combines market and media data so that the circulation performance of newspapers and selected magazines can be observed in geographic areas that conform to television viewing patterns. To do this SRDS uses the counties within the boundaries established by Nielsen for each "Designated Market Area."

Function This source offers media planners a method of determining the impact or coverage penetration of print media for well over 100 market areas in the United States. By centralizing audience penetration information for daily and Sunday newspapers, supplements, and leading national magazines within practical marketing boundaries, SRDS offers a unique reference for planning.

Planners can, for example, match areas of best sales potential with circulation, or determine which newspapers could best support shortfalls in magazine coverage. It can also suggest which markets would benefit from radio or television schedules because of limited print efforts. It is invaluable for those people coordinating national and local advertising programs.

Format Notes The measure listed as "Penetration" is calculated by dividing the publication's circulation by the DMA household total. None of the penetration figures shown are exclusive of other publications (e.g., unduplicated).

"MAC Daily" and "MAC Sunday." These columns reflect a derived statistic that combines penetration with population, household, and retail sales figures for each county in the DMA. The "20 %" feature means the newspaper must have at least 20 percent penetration for each county to be included in this column. To interpret look at the "20 % MAC Daily" listing for the *Bay City Tribune*. All of the paper's circulation (5,991) was found in a county or counties where it had at least 20 percent penetration. The paper's actual penetration of the county or counties is 45 percent, and the total households for the area where the *Tribune* had at least the minimum coverage was 13,000. Note that the *Baytown Sun*, with a circulation of more than twice that of the *Tribune*, had no county penetrations of at least 20 percent.

Illustrations A national advertiser has scheduled one page in each of two magazines for October (*TV Guide* and *Reader's Digest*). The planner wants to know how many household GRP these magazines deliver in the Houston DMA. By checking the penetration percentages at the bottom of the listing this is easily determined. The *TV Guide* receives a 10.5 penetration rating and the *Reader's Digest* receives a 15.1. The combined GRP is 25.6.

A Texas food company has scheduled an ad in four issues of the *Houston Chronicle*. The newspaper GRP goal for the DMA is 100. Does the company have to increase the schedule or add newspapers to meet its goal? Each issue of the *Chronicle* has a penetration rating of 25.2; with four issues the goal is satisfied (100.8 GRP).

TELEVISION VIEWING AREA (DMA) PRINT ANALYSIS

HOUSTON DMA (20 COUNTIES) TX

POPULATION 4,352,100   **HOUSEHOLDS** 1,553,800   **RETAIL SALES** $33,137,286,000   **AVG HSLD INC** $48,540

AUSTIN .5%, BRAZORIA 4.4%, CALHOUN .5%, CHAMBERS .5%, COLORADO .5%, FORT BEND 5.3%, GALVESTON 5.6%, GRIMES .4%, HARRIS 70.6%, JACKSON .3%, LIBERTY 1.2%, MATAGORDA .9%, MONTGOMERY 4.7%, POLK .9%, SAN JACINTO .4%, TRINITY .3%, WALKER 1.0%, WALLER .5%, WASHINGTON .6%, WHARTON .9%

	Total Daily within DMA	Pene-tration	A.M. or All Day within DMA	Pene-tration	Evening within DMA	Pene-tration	20% MAC DAILY* Circulation	Pene-tration	Hsids (000)	SUNDAY within DMA	Pene-tration	20% MAC SUNDAY Circulation	Pene-tration	Hsids (000)
★□ ANGLETON TIMES	2,229	.1%	2,229	.1%						2,929	.2%			
★□ BAY CITY TRIBUNE	5,991	.4%			5,991	.4%	5,991	45.0%	13	5,991	.4%	5,991	45.0%	13
★ BAYTOWN SUN	14,527	.9%			14,527	.9%				14,711	.9%			
BEAUMONT ENTERPRISE	2,072	.1%	2,072	.1%						2,578	.2%			
★□ BRENHAM BANNER PRESS	5,015	.3%			5,015	.3%	5,015	50.7%	10	5,015	.3%	5,015	50.7%	10
★ BRYAN-COLLEGE STATION EAGLE	974	.1%	974	.1%						1,140	.1%			
★ CONROE COURIER	12,509	.8%	12,509	.8%						13,340	.9%			
DALLAS MORNING NEWS	1,138	.1%	1,138	.1%						1,284	.1%			
★ FREEPORT-CLUTE BRAZOSPORT FACTS	18,873	1.2%			18,873	1.2%	18,873	27.4%	69	20,187	1.3%	20,187	29.3%	69
★□ GALVESTON COUNTY NEWS	25,367	1.6%	25,367	1.6%			25,367	29.2%	87	24,181	1.6%	24,181	27.8%	87
★□ HOUSTON CHRONICLE@	391,950	25.2%	391,950	25.2%			348,988	27.8%	1253	571,729	36.8%	559,334	38.0%	1473
★ HOUSTON POST	264,277	17.0%	264,277	17.0%						303,178	19.5%	229,354	20.9%	1097
★ HUNTSVILLE ITEM	5,823	.4%			5,823	.4%	5,417	33.4%	16	6,242	.4%	5,962	36.8%	16
★ PASADENA CITIZEN	7,344	.5%	7,344	.5%						7,344	.5%			
★□ ROSENBERG HERALD-COASTER	9,408	.6%			9,408	.6%				9,408	.6%			
★ TEXAS CITY SUN	9,817	.6%	9,817	.6%						10,106	.7%			
VICTORIA ADVOCATE	8,840	.6%	8,840	.6%			5,953	51.3%	12	9,290	.6%	6,309	54.4%	12
TOTAL NEWSPAPERS	786,154	50.6%	726,517	46.8%	59,637	3.8%				1,008,653	64.9%			
CE CENTEX ADI BUY	974	.1%	974	.1%		.0%				1,140	.1%			
FC FREEPORT-CLUTE BRAZOSPORT FACTS/ ANGLETON TIMES	21,102	1.4%	2,229	.1%	18,873	1.2%	18,873	27.4%	69	23,116	1.5%	20,187	29.3%	69
GT GREAT STATE OF SOUTH TEXAS GROUP	8,927	.6%	8,927	.6%		.0%	5,953	51.3%	12	9,432	.6%	6,309	54.4%	12
HO HOUSTON USSPI GROUP	74,170	4.8%	45,220	2.9%	28,950	1.9%	30,382	31.4%	97	73,999	4.8%	29,196	30.2%	97

Refer to the group listing in Section II for additional weekly circulation.

	F CIRC			F CIRC			F CIRC			F CIRC	
*4COLOR	877,798	56.5%	ANR WN	114,077	7.3%	MODMAT	299,966	19.3%	PEOPLE	55,588	3.6%
METROP	880,467	56.7%	USSPI	467,448	30.1%	MONEY	37,227	2.4%	PLABOY	54,391	3.5%
PARADE	577,289	37.2%	BET HO	102,622	6.6%	N GEOG	113,197	7.3%	POPSCI	26,377	1.7%
SUNDAY	876,331	56.4%	COSMO	45,672	2.9%	NEWSWK	45,353	2.9%	PREVNT	40,045	2.6%
USAWKD	396,133	25.5%	EBONY	44,155	2.8%	PARNTS	22,861	1.5%	R DGST	234,148	15.1%
GDHSKP	56,668	3.6%				MOMAT	56,668	3.6%	RED BK	46,688	3.6%
LHJ	68,057	6.6%				MONEY	50,201	3.2%	SO LIV	63,836	4.1%
LIFE	45,672	2.9%				N GEOG	68,057	4.4%	SPRTIL	43,927	2.8%
MCCALL	63,640	2.8%				NEWSWK	26,005	1.7%	TIME	61,609	4.0%
						PARNTS	63,640	4.1%	TV GDE	163,420	10.5%
						USNEWS	32,879	2.1%			
						WO DAY	56,284	3.6%			

Source 11
Network Television 30-Second Participation Cost Estimator
••

Description In contrast to other national media, television pricing for the four basic networks (ABC, CBS, FOX, NBC) is very volatile. Fixed pricing (published rates) for regularly scheduled programming is essentially nonexistent. Prices for participations are negotiated between each network and its marketing clients. Prices can be negotiated for one program, or for combinations; for one week, or for as long as a year's worth of television time.

To provide some guide to this fluid marketplace, advertising agencies try to compile data on past purchasing and program performance to prepare cost forecasts that are necessary for planning.

With so many variables (show popularity, audience type, seasonal trends, advertiser demand, etc.) costs are calculated for dayparts. It would be futile to create estimates for most individual shows; they change too often.

Function Cost guides are primarily used for budgeting and allocation work. They are not used in the negotiation for actual programming.

These estimators can give planners some framework for making decisions on target audience availability, reach and frequency levels, and continuity options. As a starting point, they are important.

Format Notes **"Cost Basis."** The estimator shown here is based on the foundation of all television pricing—television homes. Rating of programming begins with home viewing. Marketers desiring estimators for selected audience demographics can obtain them if the profile is measured and reported by Nielsen.

"CPR Costing." Estimates could reflect cost-per-thousands, or unit prices (actual dollars). However, planners have found it more convenient to reflect costs as dollars per rating point. Cost per rating (point) is then a multiplier. The price for one point can be multiplied by the number of GRP desired.

"Daypart Costing." As explained, costs are arranged according to the sections of the programming day. To be sure, all programs within a daypart are not equally popular, so even a price range may not capture the least valued or the highest valued programs within the time period. Though daypart costing may be rough in application, it is illogical to arrange estimators that try to be program-specific.

"Seasonal Adjustments." Historically, television media activity is not the same month after month. Most of the costing variables shift: programs change, viewer interest changes, and advertising demand changes. All these contribute to the need for seasonal price changes. What an advertiser allocates for a February schedule will not buy the same in December.

Illustration   There are at least two ways that this estimator can be used. Working *to* dollars means deciding how many GRP are needed and finding the cost. If an advertiser wanted 100 "prime" rating points during the second calendar quarter it would cost between $1,120,000 and $1,410,000 (100 × $11,200 and 100 × $14,100).

Another approach is to work *from* dollars. In this, the dollars available is a firm figure and the estimator will tell us how many GRP can be expected. If the second quarter money available for prime programming was $1,300,000, the firm might expect to purchase between 92 and 116 GRP ($1,300,000 ÷ $14,100 and $1,300,000 ÷ $11,200).

Network TV CPR Ranges (TV HH) for Selected Dayparts by Calendar Quarter ($s in Thousands)

	1st	2nd	3rd	4th
Daytime	$3.6–3.9	$3.7–4.3	$2.8–3.6	$3.9–4.5
Eve. News	$5.0–5.4	$6.6–7.1	$4.8–5.2	$6.2–6.6
Primetime	$8.5–10.4	$11.2–14.1	$9.9–12.4	$10.9–13.6
Late Night (Till 1 a.m.)	$6.5–7.8	$7.7–8.2	$7.2–7.8	$7.9–8.4

Source: Agency Estimates (compiled)

Source 12
Cable Television Network 30-Second Cost Estimator
(Nighttime)
··

Description   These estimator prices are provided by the cable networks to roughly define costs for planning. As was true for the traditional television network pricing, the prices do not reflect special programming, nor do they reflect negotiated rates. These figures are the so-called "asking prices" or "street" prices.

Function   Media planners will use such estimations in only the earliest stages of allocation and budgeting. Now that cable networks are receiving regular measurement from the Nielsen panels, it should not be long before unit pricing (per each participation) will be replaced by the standard CPR approach used elsewhere. Unfortunately, the audience selectiveness of cable network programming deserves more than just reporting popularity in broad (i.e., "mass") demographics.

Format Notes   It is worth repeating that the costs shown are unit prices and do not indicate directly any rating variations.
     The use of minimum to maximum price range reflects that at least three conditions influence prices. First, program costs to the network vary widely. Another factor involves popularity of individual programs even where the programming is of a singular nature (e.g., MTV or Headline News). Finally, prices always are influenced by advertiser demand for certain selective audiences.

Illustration   The use of unit cost estimators depends upon whether the planning is working "to dollars" or working "from dollars." To decide how many dollars are needed for a schedule, the planner should have some rating reference. The planner also needs to decide which unit cost figure would be most valid for estimation. The variations would include the highest/lowest price shown, a mean average for the range, or some composite or interpolated unit cost.
     Working from a strict budget limit still entails deciding on a single price to be divided into the dollars available. Once it is known how many participations can be purchased, the planner can apply some rating values to judge impact.

Cable TV Network 30-Second Unit Cost Rates (Selected Networks)

Network	Daytime	Primetime
A&E	$1,600–2,900	$5,800–17,000
Family	$600–2,400	$4,000–15,000
Lifetime	$1,500–3,900	$4,100–18,000
MTV	$2,500–3,500	$3,500–7,000
Nick at Nite	— —	$3,500–4,500
TNT	$2,500–3,500	$6,200–8,000
USA	$1,000–1,500	$5,000–16,000

Source: Agency Estimates (compiled)

Source 13
Spot Television 30-Second Participation Cost Estimator
....

Description Pricing for individual television market schedules, in most cases, is just as fluid as network television. With pricing based on program popularity, advertiser demand, market size, and station coverage, along with negotiation, spot television prices are even less predictable.

To make reasonable plans for schedules, media departments must monitor the changes in pricing throughout the year. This is done by using a syndicated service such as SQAD Reports, or maintaining an in-house history of television buys for each client by market.

Function Media planners use these market estimates in various ways including: market-to-market dollar allocation, costing reach levels, and determining schedule lengths. Of course, the actual prices will not be known until the television buyer completes negotiations with each station used.

Format Notes "**Cost Basis.**"   Because cost is very much a function of the program popularity (rating), spot market estimations are reported as the cost of one percent of the market's television households. In each schedule the rating of the program is divided into the cost of the announcement. All calculations are summarized into segments of the program day called dayparts. From this, reasonable averages are formed that fairly represent price forecasting.

"**Daypart Organization.**"   Because our country has multiple time zones, it is more logical to divide the broadcast day by something other than hours. The daypart concept not only reflects time, it also indicates reasonably consistent patterns of program type (e.g., "early news" and "late evening" talk shows). Broadcast planners and buyers understand that these program types tend to attract certain demographic groups of viewers.

"**Seasonal Cost Adjustment.**"   Below the market prices is a table that suggests what price adjustments should be made for different times of the year. Spot market television costs must be adjusted for when the advertiser's schedule will run. Cost per rating factors shown represent 2nd quarter (April-May-June) prices.

Illustrations As was the case in network television, planners can use these estimates to create allocations or budgets or to work within existing allocations or budgets.

Working *to* dollars means asking how much will it cost to schedule X number of rating points in Y daypart during certain quarters of the year. The answer is in dollars.

Working *from* dollars means asking how many rating points can be scheduled from X dollars in Y daypart during certain quarters of the year. The answer is in GRP that can also be translated into reach and frequency.

If the planner is working with a fixed (i.e., firm) list of markets, calculations can be done on a combined CPR. If the market list is not firm, calculations must be done for each market until the budget or allocation is exhausted.

Spot Television Cost Per Rating Point (TV Homes)
Top 50 DMA Areas (30-Second Units)

Ranked DMAs	TV HH (000)	% U.S.	Day Time	News Avg.*	Prime Time	Fringe Avg.*
			($)	($)	($)	($)
1. New York	6,716	7.0	217	607	1,207	446
2. Los Angeles	4,936	5.2	268	554	1,223	434
3. Chicago	3,102	3.3	127	371	487	196
4. Philadelphia	2,682	2.8	91	246	527	200
5. S.F.-Oak-San Jose	2,251	2.4	135	377	671	277
6. Boston	2,105	2.2	126	315	560	238
7. Washington, DC	1,876	2.0	85	229	419	193
8. Dallas-Forth Worth	1,821	1.9	73	253	375	124
9. Detroit	1,748	1.8	70	168	283	105
10. Atlanta	1,567	1.6	47	146	287	93
Total Top 10	28,804	30.2	1,238	3,266	6,040	2,306
11. Houston	1,562	1.6	86	218	331	112
12. Seattle-Tacoma	1,469	1.5	65	147	273	119
13. Cleveland	1,460	1.5	55	131	220	100
14. Minneapolis-St. Paul	1,411	1.5	53	167	207	116
15. Tampa-St. Pete-Sarasota	1,390	1.5	59	157	257	94
16. Miami-Ft. Lauderdale	1,309	1.4	85	193	349	123
17. Pittsburgh	1,151	1.2	45	105	160	80
18. Denver	1,142	1.2	49	126	193	104
19. Phoenix	1,133	1.2	71	193	255	131
20. St. Louis	1,120	1.2	38	117	164	68
Total Top 20	41,951	44.0	1,844	4,819	8,450	3,353
21. Sacramento-Stkn-Modesto	1,109	1.2	59	127	230	84
22. Orlando-Dayt Bch-Melb	983	1.0	45	127	184	84
23. Baltimore	979	1.0	45	126	220	92
24. Indianapolis	926	1.0	28	77	138	47
25. Portland, OR	920	1.0	41	84	172	62
26. Hartford-New Haven	917	1.0	47	138	185	97
27. San Diego	915	1.0	77	172	222	124
28. Charlotte	794	0.8	31	71	132	42
29. Milwaukee	789	0.8	30	101	121	58
30. Cincinnati	782	0.8	32	77	146	58
Total Top 30	51,065	53.5	2,280	5,917	10,200	4,100
31. Kansas City	781	0.8	45	106	154	66
32. Raleigh-Durham	763	0.8	24	97	134	70
33. Nashville	749	0.8	33	95	107	66
34. Columbus, OH	722	0.8	44	107	150	90
35. Greenville-Spartnbg-Ash	672	0.7	22	85	90	50
36. Buffalo	639	0.7	31	56	123	63
37. Salt Lake City	638	0.7	43	93	123	81
38. Grd Rpds-Kalmzoo-Bat Crk	634	0.7	28	73	90	55
39. San Antonio	628	0.7	30	90	94	45
40. Norfolk-Prtsmth-NewptNws	620	0.7	18	51	84	45
Total Top 40	57,911	60.7	2,598	6,771	11,347	4,731
41. New Orleans	615	0.6	23	64	83	36
42. Memphis	606	0.6	21	61	83	38
43. Oklahoma City	578	0.6	26	58	79	40
44. Harrisburg-Lanc-Leb-York	578	0.6	29	87	121	62
45. West Plm Bch-Ft.Pierce	571	0.6	39	80	115	66
46. Providence-New Bedford	567	0.6	27	68	121	58
47. Wilkes Barre-Scranton	555	0.6	17	45	77	34
48. Greensboro-Winstn Salem	548	0.6	18	54	98	34
49. Albuquerque-Sante Fe	541	0.6	32	74	82	49
50. Louisville	539	0.6	24	57	83	41
Total Top 50	63,609	66.7	2,853	7,417	12,289	5,189

Source: Agency Estimates (Compiled)

Seasonal Cost Adjustments for Spot Television 30-Second Units (per daypart)

	Calendar Quarter			
	1st	2nd	3rd	4th
Daytime	87	100	95	129
Early News	64	100	99	126
Prime Time	68	100	116	128
Late Eve.	79	100	112	124

Note: Use figures as multipliers. To find the CPR for daytime in the first quarter multiply the 2nd quarter daytime CPR by .87. To find the cost for the 4th quarter multiply by 1.29.
Source: Agency Estimates (compiled)

Source 14
Network Radio 30-Second Announcement Cost Estimators

Description Network radio has been a steady, if not spectacular, advertising medium. For marketers with wide distribution on products/services, network radio can be an efficient and effective way to cover multiple markets.

Ironically, there are many more networks in radio today than in the 1930s and 1940s when radio peaked in popularity. Keeping track of the cost alternatives is handled by broadcast buyers for agencies and buying services. While negotiation for rates is not unusual, contract pricing is less volatile than in television.

Function Use of any cost estimators in broadcast is for reference purposes only. Final prices and CPR (cost per rating point) are a function of each contract. Firms considering network radio need some parameters for planning decisions, and this is why the data is compiled.

Format Notes Two cost excerpts are shown for network radio. The first is a sample of quoted prices from some popular network options. The excerpt at the bottom is a cost per rating point summary for a composite of networks based on RADAR measures. Here are some other explanations to help use these sources.

"**Affl.**" Affiliates are stations that are contractually obligated to carry at least some of the network's programming. As a rule of thumb, assume only one affiliate per market (800 affiliates would mean 800 market areas).

"**R.O.S.**" Run-of-schedule prices are the lowest encountered in broadcast buying. The literal meaning is that the network has complete control of the days and times of the marketer's schedule. In practice, this is negotiated, and advertisers are usually able to have the schedule times desired.

"**Cost per Point.**" The costs are based on yearly averages. This is logical because network radio does not show the strong seasonal shifts in price that television does. Planners do indicate, however, that pricing in the first calendar quarter is lower than average while the second quarter is higher.

Illustrations Because you have unit prices as well as cost per rating point, estimates can work to the dollars allocated or to a reach/frequency goal.

"**Unit Price Example.**" How many 30-second units can be bought from CNN + for an allocation of $85,000? Divide the allocation by the unit cost of $9,500 and the answer is nine 30-second units.

"**Cost Per Rating Point Example.**" A marketer desires an adult male target audience, and it takes 75 weekly GRP to achieve the desired reach and frequency. How many weeks of network radio can be bought for $720,000?

For morning drive time the cost per point ($3,200) is multiplied by 75. This is a weekly cost of $240,000. At this rate, three weeks are affordable ($720,000 ÷ $240,000 = 3.1 weeks).

Network Radio Prices 30-Second Commercials (for selected networks)

Network	No. Affl.	Cost/Commercial (R.O.S.)
ABC-ESPN	286	$700–$3,000
Rush Limbaugh	657	7,000
CNN +	1,199	9,500
Westwood One	5,500	1,000–15,000

Network Radio Cost per Rating Point for Selected Demographics 30-Second Commercials

Audience	M–F 6–10AM	M–F 4–7PM	Sat/Sun
Adults	$3,000	$2,800	$2,200
Adult Men	$3,000	$2,850	$2,100
Adult Women	$2,900	$2,800	$2,150
Teens	$2,140	$1,600	$1,900

Source: Agency Estimates (compiled)

Source 15
Spot Market Radio Cost Estimators (30-Second Units)
. . . .

Description   Because most U.S. cities and towns have multiple station coverage, planning and buying of spot market radio is labor-intensive. Network options can satisfy those looking for efficient ways to use radio, but for many advertisers the market-by-market approach is preferable.

With the heavy levels of price negotiation, accurate costs for radio time can only be derived from recent history. Monitoring of prices from each purchase by agencies or buying services is essential. Further, in markets where there is consistent audience measurement, costs should be expressed in cost per rating point (CPR). There is too much unit price variation between stations to report average unit prices.

Function   It is common to find spot radio estimates in two forms: by individual market or by market ranking groups. This appears to reflect different uses of the price materials.

The market-by-market prices are compiled for active radio buying accounts. This data gives negotiators better parameters in station selection.

The market group costs are best suited for planners who are comparing costs across media, or comparing spot market with network options. Group position of a market is based upon either its metropolitan population or marketing area (DMA).

Format Notes   The excerpts shown are self-explanatory, but some reminders are worthwhile.

For each market group after the first ten, the cost figure is cumulative. This means the "top 20" cost has combined the cost for 1 through 10 (shown) with the cost for markets 11 through 20.

The cost shown is for one demographic rating point in each of the markets in the group (i.e., a summary cost).

It is up to the people who compile the contract information to know how many different stations are used for a market estimate. Active buyers might only use prices from regularly used stations. Others would prefer market estimates based on all stations that fit in some sort of "mainstream" definition such as consistent popularity. Still others might prefer an estimate based on the top three or four stations in share of audience.

Illustrations   A planner for a woman's product wants to compare radio network costs with spot market costs. She estimates the cost per point for a target of adult females (18 to 34 years) to be $3,000 for national networks. How many markets (starting at the top) are affordable on a market-by-market basis? According to group estimates, the top 40 markets would cost $3,082 per point.

Another planner wants to estimate a buy made up of Eastern seaboard markets (NYC, Boston, Philadelphia, Washington, and Baltimore). The target is males 18 to 34. What is the cost for 50 GRP per week? The answer is summing the CPRs for the markets ($221 + 102 + 80 + 108 + 69 = $580 per point).

Spot Market Radio by Groups Cost/Rating for Demographics (based on 60-second commercial costs)

Metro Markets	Men			Women			Teens
	18 +	18–34	25–54	18 +	18–34	25–54	
Top 10	$1,795	$1,330	$1,824	$1,770	$1,428	$1,782	$1,128
Top 20	2,687	2,002	2,693	2,623	2,150	2,658	1,692
Top 30	3,407	2,538	3,426	3,306	2,679	3,335	2,151
Top 40	3,950	2,927	3,981	3,823	3,082	3,835	2,441
Top 50	4,336	3,219	4,391	4,253	3,408	4,239	2,646
Top 60	4,699	3,486	4,751	4,593	3,674	4,578	2,903
Top 70	5,020	3,705	5,061	4,871	3,909	4,858	3,091
Top 80	5,310	3,908	5,350	5,114	4,128	5,156	3,289
Top 90	5,440	4,117	5,585	5,319	4,310	5,378	3,431
Top 100	5,708	4,317	5,863	5,506	4,528	5,631	3,646

Source: Agency Estimates (compiled)

Top 50 DMA Spot Market Radio Cost/Rating for Demographics (based on 60-second commercial costs)

Metro Rank	Men			Women			Teens
	18 +	18–34	25–54	18 +	18–34	25–54	
1. New York	$297	$221	$291	$316	$231	$289	$186
2. Los Angeles	331	245	347	323	273	325	203
3. Chicago	173	132	183	164	132	171	133
4. San Francisco	226	186	246	236	194	260	146
5. Philadelphia	118	80	125	121	99	125	88
6. Detroit	99	70	112	95	75	99	64
7. Boston	139	102	144	126	121	144	63
8. Houston	123	71	91	90	70	85	61
9. Washington	151	108	150	155	112	150	96
10. Dallas	138	115	135	134	121	134	88
11. Miami	97	71	92	90	67	88	56
12. Nassau/Suffolk	114	79	102	106	93	101	70
13. Atlanta	134	92	126	117	96	118	72
14. Pittsburgh	54	38	59	51	47	59	35
15. St. Louis	62	52	58	61	61	65	44
16. Baltimore	81	69	83	78	63	76	52
17. Seattle	101	72	101	90	75	97	56
18. Minneapolis	63	48	65	71	54	72	17
19. San Diego	109	96	105	116	109	130	109
20. Cleveland	77	55	78	73	57	70	53
21. Tampa	77	56	78	72	54	70	54
22. Denver	91	69	92	88	65	88	59
23. Phoenix	88	65	90	82	66	179	56
24. Portland, OR	74	55	76	71	56	67	42
25. Milwaukee	51	36	53	48	36	46	32
26. Kansas City	47	34	47	45	35	45	29
27. Providence	63	49	67	61	46	60	40
28. San Jose	125	94	129	117	91	115	73
29. Cincinnati	47	37	45	47	39	55	38
30. New Orleans	57	41	56	52	41	52	36
31. Sacramento	72	51	69	70	61	68	45
32. Norfolk	46	32	50	48	40	50	23
33. Columbus, OH	54	41	57	47	38	48	18
34. Buffalo	42	29	39	38	30	37	26
35. Salt Lake City	44	29	47	42	32	41	31
36. Indianapolis	51	38	53	51	43	49	17
37. San Antonio	43	31	42	41	34	39	20
38. Riverside	57	43	60	55	34	41	18
39. Hartford	87	62	91	79	58	84	71
40. Charlotte	47	33	47	46	33	43	21
41. Rochester, NY	50	24	51	56	31	50	29
42. Oklahoma City	28	19	27	30	21	28	18
43. Louisville	31	25	33	33	33	32	15
44. Dayton	37	26	39	38	31	34	24
45. Birmingham	41	30	41	47	30	45	27
46. Nashville	50	35	53	48	37	48	17
47. Greensboro	29	18	30	38	28	34	23
48. Memphis	41	31	43	41	30	43	24
49. Orlando	51	39	52	57	44	51	28
50. Albany, NY	28	45	41	42	41	39	N/A

Source: Agency Estimates (compiled)

Source 16
Major Market Daily Newspaper Cost and Coverage Estimator

Description   Newspaper market cost planners are designed as a quick reference for those firms considering print advertising in multiple cities.

The costs reflect the standard advertising unit (SAU) width (2.06 inches) by one inch in depth. The costs often reflect more than one daily newspaper in each market. This is needed to balance the uneven coverage that would be provided from a single newspaper in each market area.

Function   These estimators provide quick answers to those who are involved with budgeting and/or allocation of dollars. Because they do not indicate any discount or volume incentives, their value is confined to the early stages of cost consideration. For contract purposes buyers will deal with each publication's rate schedule.

Format Notes   "**Adult Daily Coverage.**"   The figures shown on the excerpt reflect Scarborough measurements of adult readership on an average issue basis. The geographic boundary of DMA best fits the planning of national or regional marketers.

"**Gross Coverage.**"   Where the coverage figure is followed by "G" the readership estimate will include duplicated adults (those that read more than one of the papers included).

"**Net Coverage.**"   Where the coverage figure is followed by "N" the estimate is net or unduplicated readers. Such figures are usually available where a publishing company owns two or more of the market's newspapers and offers them in combination.

"**Scope of Market List.**"   The excerpt lists only the 10 largest market areas. Rate information is available for all markets that accept SAU policies. Adult reader coverage figures are limited by the range of Scarborough surveys (top 50 markets is a rule of thumb).

Illustration   For working to dollars the planner must know the size of the ad(s) so that the column inches needed is fixed. The identification of market areas is also necessary. If a planner wanted to know the open cost of 1,000 column inches in Boston and Washington, the rates ($249 + $406) would be added ($655) and multiplied by 1,000. The answer is $655,000.

For working from a budget or allocation, the buyer must know the market or markets desired. To reverse the situation above, an allocation of $500,000 is available for Boston and Washington. For equal schedules in both areas, the dollars would be divided by the column inch rates for both markets ($655). The answer (763 SAU column inches) shows the advertising space affordable in both markets.

Daily Newspaper Costs and Coverage for the Top 10 U.S. DMAs

Market	Adult DMA Cov.	Newspapers	$/SAU Column Inch
New York	36% (G)	2	$756
Los Angeles	28	1	502
Chicago	29	1	400
Philadelphia	31 (N)	2	370
San Francisco	30 (N)	2	335
Boston	33	1	249
Washington	50	1	406
Dallas	34	1	258
Detroit	34	1	435
Houston	36	1	252

Notes: ''G'' means gross or duplicated coverage.
''N'' means net or unduplicated coverage from morning and evening newspaper combinations.
Source: Audit Bureau of Circulation and Standard Rate and Data

Source 17
Standard Rate and Data Service (SRDS) Newspaper Rates and Data
. . . .

Research Company   Standard Rate and Data Service (SRDS)

Description   This service covers most all individual market media. It is a catalog concept that is published monthly to provide directory-type listings for each market's media.

For most local market media, the SRDS listing covers: contact numbers (phone/FAX), pricing data, production basics, and other things that would assist media planners and buyers.

Function   For those planners and buyers outside of the home market this is the fastest and most accurate reference for evaluation and selection. Newspaper buyers learn to master the alpha system quickly (by state by city). Further, because all the listings follow the same format, fast access to key information for comparisons is simple.

Format Notes   "Rates."   The Springfield newspaper accepts the SAU national format and charges by the column inch or by page units. Discounts ("Newsplan-SAU" under section 5) are offered for pages used per year or the equivalent in column inches.

"Color Charges."   Newspapers are fairly consistent in charges for color advertising units. The Springfield newspaper shows a surcharge (over and above the column inch cost). Do not confuse this charge with the color rates for Sunday Comics (section 18). Comics color charges are usually included with space charges.

Illustration   If the buyer has the proposed schedule (frequency and ad sizes) there is little mystery in finding the correct cost. Suppose the newspaper was scheduled for 13 black and white units (3 columns wide by 7 inches deep). First calculate the number of column inches involved. Each unit is 21 inches (3 × 7). There are 13 insertions so total inches is 273 (21 × 13). Discounts do *not* begin until 774 inches are contracted for so the applicable rate is either $49.84 (Monday through Saturday) or $56.20 for Sunday insertions. Multiply to find either the per-insertion cost or the total cost.

Springfield

Hampden County—Map Location C-5

UNION-NEWS
REPUBLICAN
Newhouse Newspapers
P.O. Box: 1131, 1860 Main St., Springfield, MA 01101.
Phone 413-788-1050. Fax: 413-788-1199.

ABC

Location ID: 1 NSNL MA   Mid 016727-000
Member: INAME; NAB, Inc; ABC Coupon Distribution Ver-
ification Service; ACB, Inc.
Union-News—MORNING.
Republican—SUNDAY.

1. PERSONNEL
Pub—David Starr.
Adv Dir—Dwight L. Brouillard.
Natl Adv Mgr—Joseph V. Ascioti.

2. REPRESENTATIVES and/or BRANCH OFFICES
Newhouse Newspapers—Metro-Suburbia, Inc.

3. COMMISSION AND CASH DISCOUNT
15% to agencies; 2% 15th following month.

4. POLICY-ALL CLASSIFICATIONS
30-day notice given of any rate revision.
Alcoholic beverage advertising accepted.

ADVERTISING RATES
Effective October 1, 1992.
Received August 3, 1992.

5. BLACK/WHITE RATES

	Morn.	Sun.
SAU open, per inch	49.84	56.20

Inches charged full depth: col. 21.5; pg. 129; dbl. truck
279.5.
NEWSPLAN—SAU

Pages	% Disc.	Morn.	Sun.	Inches
6	2	48.84	55.08	774
13	4	47.84	53.93	1,677
26	8	45.84	51.71	3,354
52	18	40.87	46.08	6,708
78	20	39.87	44.96	10,062

See Newsplan Contract and Copy Regulations—items 3,
4, 5, 6, 7, 8, 10, 11, 13, 14, 15, 17.

7. COLOR RATES AND DATA
B/w 1 c, min. 28 col. inches; b/w 2 c and 3 c, min. 48 col.
inches.
Use b/w rate plus the following applicable costs:

	b/w 1 c	b/w 2 c	b/w 3 c
Extra	632.00	933.00	1,231.00

9. SPLIT RUN
Available Monday and Tuesday.   No color available.
Normal composition charge for type A/B perfect split,
extra 135.00 flat charge.

11. SPECIAL DAYS/PAGES/FEATURES
Best Food Day: Wednesday.
Weekend Section: Thursday; Leisure Time (Travel): Sun-
day.

12. R.O.P. DEPTH REQUIREMENTS
Ads over 20 inches deep charged full col.

13. CONTRACT AND COPY REGULATIONS
See Contents page for locations of regulation—items 1, 6,
13, 18, 25.

14. CLOSING TIME
Published Morning and Sunday.

Day	Time Closes	Day	Time Closes
Mon	...	Thu Fri	... Tue
Tue	...	Fri Sat	... Wed
Wed	...	Fri Sun	... Wed
Thu	...	Mon	

SPECIAL SECTION

Day	Time Closes
Travel (Sun)	*

(*) 9 days before publication.

15. MECHANICAL MEASUREMENTS
PRINTING   PROCESS: Photo Composition Direct
Lithography.
6 col; ea 2-1/16˝; 1/8˝ betw col.
Inches charged full depth: col. 21.5; pg. 129; dbl. truck
279.5.

16. SPECIAL CLASSIFICATIONS/RATES
Amusements—general rates applies.
POSITION CHARGES
Next to reading 12-1/2%; full position 25%. Minimum for
position 2 co. inches. Specified page not guaranteed.

17. CLASSIFIED RATES
For complete data refer to classified rate section.

18. COMICS
POLIC—ALL CLASSIFICATIONS
When orders are placed through Metro-Puck Comics
Network—see that listing.
Received November 4, 1992.
COLOR RATES AND DATA

1 page	6,141.00	1/3 page	2,937.00
2/3 page	4,909.00	1/6 page	2,077.00
1/2 page	3,799.00		

CLOSING TIMES
23 days before publication.
MECHANICAL MEASUREMENTS
PRINTING PROCESS: Offset.
Page size 13˝ wide x 20˝ deep; 7 cols. to page.
Send repro proofs to Treasure Chest Advertising Co.,
7619 Doane Dr., Manassas, VA. 22110.

20. CIRCULATION
Union-News, per copy .35. Sunday Republican, per copy
1.25.
Net Paid—A.B.C. 9-30-92 (Newspaper Form)

	Total	CZ	TrZ	Other
Morn	109,558	76,681	26,573	6,304
Sun	157,278	101,060	43,608	12,610

A.B.C. Zip Code Analysis available from publisher.
For county, MSA & ADI data, see CIRCULATION 93.

Newspaper Rates and Data

Source 18
SRDS Consumer Magazine and Agri-Media Rates and Data
....

Research Company   Standard Rates and Data Service (SRDS)

Description   This service covers most all regularly scheduled magazines (national and regional). Essentially a catalog, SRDS publishes this reference to provide directory-type listings for each publication.

For magazines, the SRDS listing covers: contact numbers (phone/FAX), editorial description, pricing data, production basics, and other things that would assist media planners and buyers.

Function   For planners and buyers this is a fast and accurate source for preliminary evaluation. SRDS arranges the magazine listings into discrete editorial categories much as a telephone Yellow Pages might do. It then lists magazines by an alpha system. Further, magazine planners can compare information quickly; because all the listings follow the same format, fast access to key information for comparisons is simple.

Format Notes   "Rates."   Magazines traditionally sell space by the page or fraction of a page. Rates and volume discounts are thus arranged by the number of insertions used in a contract year.

"Color Charges."   Unlike newspapers, color is included in the rates for most magazines listed in SRDS (i.e., instead of a color surcharge). Section 6 in each SRDS listing will explain, but be sure to read carefully.

"Combination" and "Network Discounts."   A significant number of consumer magazines are published by companies that offer multiple titles to the public. Magazine planners who are considering other titles from the same publisher must check the network discounts to find the lowest applicable prices.

"Cover Prices."   Somewhat unique to magazines is the availability of cover positions for advertising. There are three such positions for possible sale (the front cover is for magazine identification). The second cover is the inside of the front cover. The third cover immediately precedes the back or 4th cover. Covers usually command premium prices because of their visibility. They also tend to be used by the same advertiser for extended periods (more than one year).

Illustration   While magazines tend to design their pricing based on the frequency use, planners using SRDS to estimate costs must be careful to interpret the price schedule correctly.

Suppose a planner was trying to cost out a proposed schedule for *Skin Diver*. Here is the proposed use of space for the year:

12 black and white insertions (9 pages and 3 half-pages)
3 four-color pages

What prices are correct for the black and white schedule? Though there are 12 insertions, the rate card says that smaller units (e.g., the half-page sizes) cannot increase the frequency discount of the larger ads. However, the page units (9) can be combined with smaller units. Translation: the 9 page insertions will use the "9 ti." price of $7,750. The half-page units (3) are entitled to the "12 ti." rate of $4,550 (9 + 3 = 12).

Can the color schedule (3 pages) be combined with the black and white units? No. As the last line of section 5 is written: *"Insertions of different rate classifications may not be combined for discounts."* The color discount price of $12,935 is the correct price for the color pages.

A Petersen Publishing Co. Publication

ABC   MPA

Location ID: 8 MLST 45   Mld 001127-000
Published monthly by Petersen Publishing Co., 8490
Sunset Blvd., Los Angeles, CA 90069. Phone 310-854-
2222.
For shipping info., see Print Media Production Data.

PUBLISHER'S EDITORIAL PROFILE

SKIN DIVER's editorial package can be broken into 3
basic categories: news, safety and education; product and
performance reports; and travel—both domestic and in-
ternational. Features and columns cover various areas of
underwater recreation, with diving sites that range from
local and regional, to places such as the Caribbean,
Hawaii, Micronesia, the Seychelles, and the Sea of
Cortez. Rec'd 12/29/88.

1. PERSONNEL
Sr VP/Corp Mktg/Sales—Peter F. Clancey.
VP/Grp Pub/Marine Photography—Paul Tzimoulis.
Pub—Bill Gleason.
Assoc Pub—Carolyn Pascal.

2. REPRESENTATIVES and/or BRANCH OFFICES
Los Angeles, CA 90069—8490 Sunset Blvd. Phone 310-
854-2222. FAX: 310-854-1556.
Atlanta, GA 30305—4 Piedmont Center, Suite 601. Phone
404-231-4004. FAX: 404-233-6982.
Chicago, IL 60610—The Petersen Building, 815 N.
LaSalle St. Phone 312-649-0660. FAX: 312-649-6621.
Irving (Dallas), TX 75062—800 W. Airport Freeway, Suite
201. Phone 214-579-0454. FAX: 214-579-0589.

Detroit, MI 48226—333 West Fort St. Bldg., Suite 1800.
Phone 313-964-6680. FAX: 313-964-4139.
New York, NY 10022—437 Madison Ave. Phone 212-
935-9150. FAX: 212-319-8443.

3. COMMISSION AND CASH DISCOUNT
15% to recognized agencies. No cash discount. Net 30
days.

4. GENERAL RATE POLICY
Rates subject to change upon notice from publisher.
Advertising will be billed at rates then prevailing. Advertisers will be short-rated or credited, if within their 12
consecutive month contract period they use an amount of
space or number of insertions that earn rate different from
rate at which they have ben billed.
All verbal insertions regarding contracts or insertions must
be confirmed in writing.

ADVERTISING RATES
Effective January 1, 1992. (issue) (Card No. 40)
Rates received August 13, 1991.

5. BLACK/WHITE RATES

	1 ti	3 ti	6 ti	9 ti	12 ti
1 page	8,335.	8,085.	7,920.	7,750.	7,585.
2/3 page	6,335.	6,145.	6,020.	5,890.	5,765.
1/2 page	5,000.	4,850.	4,750.	4,650.	4,550.
1/3 page	3,750.	3,640.	3,565.	3,490.	3,415.
1/4 page	2,915.	2,830.	2,770.	2,710.	2,655.
1/6 page	2,085.	2,020.	1,980.	1,940.	1,895.
1/12 page	1,125.	1,090.	1,070.	1,045.	1,025.
1 inch	458.	444.	435.	426.	417.
Agate line	32.72	31.72	31.08	30.43	29.79

FREQUENCY DISCOUNTS
Discounts are determined by the total number of insertions used during a contract year. Schedules composed
of mixed space units are entitled to frequency discounts
except when use of smaller units lowers total cost of
campaign below amount which larger units reached at
their earned rate. Rate holders unacceptable. Insertions
of different rate classifications may not be combined for
discounts. Inserts contribute to discounts on a pro-rated
basis, but do not earn discounts.

BULK DISCOUNTS
Available to General Rate advertisers in lieu of frequency
for 18 or more pages or the fractional equivalent run
during a contract year.
18 pages .... 12%   36 pages 18%
24 pages 14%

5a. COMBINATION RATES
Petersen Magazine Network discount:
Available to any General Rate advertiser who runs a
minimum of 2 pages in each of 3 titles (6 pages) during a
12-issue contract year. A 1 page minimum is required in
each additional title. Petersen Magazine Network discount is earned in lieu of all other discounts, based on
cumulative gross revenue run in all qualifying Petersen
Magazine Network titles. Minimum 1/3 page. Contract
required. Also see Petersen Magazine Network listing
under classification No. 30.

6. COLOR RATES

	1 ti	3 ti	6 ti	9 ti	12 ti
Black and 1-Color:					
1 page	10,420.	10,105.	9,900.	9,690.	9,480.
2/3 page	8,130.	7,885.	7,725.	7,560.	7,400.
1/2 page	6,460.	6,265.	6,135.	6,010.	5,880.
1/3 page	5,000.	4,850.	4,750.	4,650.	4,550.
	1 ti	3 ti	6 ti	9 ti	12 ti
4-Color:					
1 page	13,335.	12,935.	12,670.	12,400.	12,135.
2/3 page	10,670.	10,350.	10,135.	9,925.	9,710.
1/2 page	8,670.	8,410.	8,235.	8,065.	7,890.
1/3 page	7,335.	7,115.	6,970.	6,820.	6,675.

7. COVERS

	1 ti	3 ti	6 ti	9 ti	12 ti
4-Color:					
2nd cover	14,585.	14,145.	13,855.	13,565.	13,270.
3rd cover	13,335.	12,935.	12,670.	12,400.	12,135.
4th cover	15,420.	14,955.	14,650.	14,340.	14,030.

8. INSERTS
Available.

9. BLEED
No charge.

10. SPECIAL POSITION
Publisher reserves the right to give better position than
specified. Inside covers may be preempted at the Publisher's discretion.

14. CONTRACT AND COPY REGULATIONS
See Contents page for location—items 2, 3, 7, 8, 9, 10,
12, 18, 20, 24, 30, 32, 33, 34, 35, 36, 37, 39.

15. GENERAL REQUIREMENTS
Also see SRDS Print Media Production Data.
Printing Process: Web offset Full Run Regional
Cover
Trim Size: 7-7/8 x 10-1/2; No./Cols. 3.
Binding Method: Perfect.
Colors Available: Black and white; Black and one
color; 4-color process; Matched; 5 COL.
Covers: 4-color process.

AD PAGE DIMENSIONS

1 pg 6-3/4 x 9-5/8	1/4 h 4-1/2 x 3-5/8
2/3 v 4-1/2 x 9-5/8	1/6 v 2-1/8 x 4-3/4
1/2 v 4-1/2 x 7-1/4	1/6 h 4-1/2 x 2-1/4
1/2 h 6-3/4 x 4-3/4	1/12 h 2-1/8 x 2-1/4
1/3 v 2-1/8 x 9-5/8	1 in 2-1/8 x 1
1/3 sq 4-1/2 x 4-3/4	
Gut Bleed Sprd 14-1/2 x 9-5/8	

Source 19
SRDS Spot Television Rates and Data

Research Company   Standard Rate and Data Service (SRDS)

Description   As with previous SRDS sources, the data and information on each commercial television station is published monthly throughout the year. What it intends to do is to provide all the pertinent facts media buyers and others need to make fair judgments about each station in a television market.

Unfortunately, many television stations no longer submit any advertising rate information to SRDS. Published rates for television time need stability to be worthwhile to buyers, and this is less and less likely in the changing world of television. In an era of negotiated prices, published rates would be inaccurate before SRDS even received them from the station.

Some stations, however, are willing to submit prices for television time, and for these SRDS is valuable.

Function   There is no standard format for pricing time. Each station is at complete liberty to arrange its rate information any way it wishes. Part of the value of this edition of SRDS is to educate time buyers on each station's approach to selling time. In addition, SRDS listings inform buyers on scheduling policies, contract restrictions, and some production capabilities. If the station complies fully, the time buyer has a fast, efficient reference for each television station.

Format Notes   The excerpt shown on the next page is only one of a variety of rate formats. It does represent a popular option known as a "grid" approach that establishes program-by-program prices while still offering negotiation flexibility.

Note that each program has five price options. Here is how the grid functions:

Column "F."   The letter "F" stands for "Fixed." This means advertisers willing to pay this price will not be shifted from the commercial position. It also suggests that advertisers paying this rate have some choice on the location of the commercial within the program.

Note that this is the highest price for each program. For extremely popular shows this may be acceptable, but many buyers will try for lower prices.

Column "P-1."   According to station notes this price level will not be preempted by a fixed rate buyer. The assumption is that "P-1" does not have the scheduling flexibility shown to "Fixed" price buyers, but it is permitted to preempt all 2, 3, or 4 level positions.

Columns "P2-P4."   The "P-2" through "P-4" prices represent "preemptible" prices. These are progressively lower than the fixed rate because there is risk involved with these commercial positions. If a buyer accepts preemptible prices, the client may lose the position to an advertiser willing to pay a higher price. The ranking 2 through 4 refers to the length of notice the station will give you before "evicting" the advertiser. In many cases, those gambling on the P4 prices might not receive *any* prior notice from the station. Stations who are forced to move advertisers will try to find good substitutes for positions lost, but there are no expressed guarantees.

WIS-TV
(Airdate November 7, 1953)
COLUMBIA

hrp HARRINGTON, RIGHTER & PARSONS, INC.

NAB BROADCASTERS · **TVB**

Cosmos Broadcasting Corporation Station

Location ID: 6 TLST SC   Mid 007767-000
Cosmos Broadcasting Corp.
1111 Bull St, Columbia, SC 29201. Phone 803-799-1010,
   TWX, 810-666-2636. FAX: 803-799-2171, .
Mailing Address: Box: 367, Columbia, SC 29202.

1. PERSONNEL
Gen Mgr—Ron Loewen.
Gen Sales Mgr—David A. Harbert.

2. REPRESENTATIVES
Harrington, Righter & Parsons, Inc.

3. FACILITIES
Video 316,000 w., audio 63,200 w.; ch 10. Stereo.
Antenna ht.: 1546 ft. above average terrain.
Operating schedule: 6:20-2:15 am Mon-Fri; 6:30-2 am Sat
& Sun. EST.

4. AGENCY COMMISSION
15% to recognized agencies on net time, except as
specified in contract.

5. GENERAL ADVERTISING REGULATIONS
General: 2a, 2b, 3a, 3c, 4a, 5, 7b, 8.
Rate Protection: 13k.
Contracts: 20c, 21, 22a, 22c, 26, 29, 31a.
Basic Rates: 40a, 40b, 41b, 41c, 42, 43a, 46, 47, 47d,
47k.
Comb.; Cont. Discounts: 60a, 60d, 60e, 60f, 62c.
Cancellation: 70b, 70h, 71, 72, 73a, 73b.
Prod. Services: 80, 82, 83, 84, 85, 86, 87b.
Rates offered herein are for the product of a single
company only.
Multiple Product Announcement
Piggyback commercials of less than 60 seconds duration
are not acceptable.
Affiliated with NBC Television Network.

6. TIME RATES
No. 91-2 Effective January 25, 1991.
Received February 4, 1991.

7. SPOT ANNOUNCEMENTS

	F	P1	P2	P3	P4
MON THRU FRI, AM:					
6:00, Early Riser	100	80	60	40	25
6:15-7, News at Sunrise	170	140	120	110	100
*7-9, Today Show	300	220	190	170	150
*9-10, Peoples Court/					
Trump Card	110	80	60	50	40
9-noon, AM Rotation	110	80	70	50	40
PM:					
Noon-12:30, Mid Day					
Report	200	130	110	100	90
12:30-1, Carolina Today	100	80	70	60	50
*1-4, NBC Soaps	300	250	230	210	190
*4-5, Cosby/227	300	250	200	175	140
5-5:30, Wheel of Fortune	400	350	300	220	180
5:30-6, Jeopardy	400	350	300	250	180
6-6:30, Carolina Report	800	700	600	525	450
6:30-7, NBC Nightly News	700	600	500	450	400
*7-7:30, 7 O'Clock Report	1300	900	800	700	650
*7:30-8, Entertainment					
Tonight	1200	800	650	550	450
11-11:30, 11 O'Clock					
Report	1200	800	650	550	450
*11-11:30 Mon thru Sun,					
11 O'Clock Report	1200	800	650	550	450
11:30 pm-12:30 am,					
Tonight Show	160	120	100	90	80
*12:30-1:30 am, David					
Letterman	100	50	40	35	30
1:30-2 am, Bob Costas	60	50	40	35	25
*1:30-2 am Fri, Friday					
Night Videos	90	70	50	30	25
SAT, AM:					
*7:30-8, Mr. Knozit	120	100	85	75	60
8 am-12:30 pm, Kids					
Rotation	350	300	250	200	150
PM:					
12:30-1, Inside Stuff/NBA					
Magazine	350	300	250	200	150
1-6, Sports/Various	350	300	250	200	150
6-6:30, Awareness	150	120	100	80	60
6:30-7, NBC Nightly News	400	320	280	250	200
*7-7:30, 7 O'Clock Report	400	320	280	250	200
7:30-8, Newswatch	300	180	150	120	90
*11:30-1, Saturday Nite					
Live	400	300	200	160	140
1-2 am, Showtime at the					
Apollo	150	100	80	60	50
SUN, AM:					
*6:30-7, Mr. Knozit	110	90	75	50	30
7-7:30, Wild Kingdom					
7:30-9, Religous Rotation	150	130	110	80	50
9-10:30, Sunday Today	170	130	100	90	40
*10:30-11, Meet The Press	180	150	120	90	75
11-11:30, Bob Villa	180	140	110	90	75
11:30-noon, Hornet's					
Magazine	180	140	100	80	60
PM:					
Noon-12:30, George					
Felton Show	180	140	100	80	60
12:30-6, Various	500	400	300	250	225
6-6:30, 6 O'Clock News	400	320	280	250	200
*6:30-7, NBC News	500	400	300	250	225
11:30-midnight, 227	200	140	120	100	80
Midnight-12:30 am, Voices					
of America	200	140	120	100	80
AM:					
1-1:30 am, Siskel & Ebert	170	130	100	80	60
1:30-2, Memories—Then					
and Now	170	130	100	80	60
2-3, Entertainment Tonight	170	130	100	80	60

PRIME TIME

	F	P1	P2	P3	P4
MON:					
*8-9, Fresh Prince/					
Blossom	1300	1100	900	750	600
*9-11, Monday Night At					
The Movies	1600	1200	1100	900	800
TUES:					
*8-9, Matlock	3000	2200	1900	1700	1400
9-10, Heat of the Night	2200	1900	1700	1400	1200
*10-11, Law & Order	2000	1700	1400	1200	1000
WED:					
*8-9, Unsolved Mysteries	1900	1400	1200	1000	800
9-10, Fanelli Boys/Dear					
John	1900	1400	1200	1000	800
*10-11, Hunter	1900	1400	1200	1000	800
THURS:					
*8-9, Cosby Show/					
Different World	3000	2200	1900	1600	1300
9-10, Cheers/Grand	2200	1900	1600	1300	1100
*10-11, L.A. Law	1900	1600	1300	1100	900
FRI:					
*8-9, Quantum Leap	1300	1100	900	800	600
9-10, Dark Shadows	1300	1100	900	800	500
*10-11, Midnight Caller	1300	1100	900	800	600
SAT:					
*8-9, Amen/Fanelli Boys	1700	1500	1300	1000	800
9-10, Golden Girls/Empty					
Nest	2200	1900	1600	1300	1100
*10-11, Carol & Co/					
American Dreamer	2200	1900	1600	1300	1100
SUN:					
7-8, Sunday Best	1300	1100	900	800	500
8-9, Real Life W/Pauley/					
Expose	1300	1100	900	800	500
*9-11, NBC Movie	1900	1400	1200	1000	800

(*) 10 sec available.
60 sec: 2 x 30 sec.
15 sec: 80% of 30 sec.
10 sec: 70% of 30 sec.
F—Fixed, not preemptible.
P2-P4—Preemptible by higher rate.

11. SPECIAL FEATURES
COLOR
Schedules network color, slides, tape and live.
Equipped with 3/4" cassette; 1" reel; 2" reel; Beta SP &
D2; closed caption.

13. CLOSING TIME
72 hours prior film and slides; 1 week artwork; 72 hours
live instruction, script and props.

Source 20
Outdoor Billboards (Thirty-Sheet) Cost Estimator
· ·

Research Company   Outdoor Advertising Association of America (OAAA)

Description   The data and information for out-of-home estimates for ''30-Sheet Format'' billboards is supplied by individual firms servicing each of the metro market areas. Where more than one posting company competes in a metro area, costs and coverage are combined to estimate market figures.

    Similar estimates are also available for other out-of-home techniques: 8-sheets, bulletins, and rotary bulletins. The 30-sheet, however, is the most common size for this type of advertising.

Function   This is a planning reference, and not usable for budgeting. It is a rough, but fast and easy way to allocate dollars for outdoor purposes. More accurate poster numbers and costs are found through negotiation with the individual posting companies.

Format Notes   The estimates on the facing page are based on 50 GRP per day. For reference, SMRB estimates that a 30-day schedule of 50 GRP will reach 80 to 85 percent, at a monthly average frequency of 12 to 17.

    The number of locations needed for 50 GRP across markets must vary because of the availability of real estate and the visual access to traffic. In most markets illuminated billboards are much more available than non-illuminated.

Outdoor Billboard Monthly Costs 50 GRP Showings for 30-Sheet Units Top 10 Market Areas

Market Area	Number of Poster Locations	Monthly Cost
New York	322	$215,700
Los Angeles	504	345,200
Chicago	217	128,100
Philadelphia	246	114,400
San Francisco	141	168,700
Boston	170	106,300
Washington	99	80,900
Dallas	59	32,500
Detroit	90	64,800
Houston	110	60,500

Source: O.A.A.A.

Media Audience Reach Estimators

Source 21
Spot Market Television Audience Reach Estimator

Description   While "reach" (unduplicated exposure over time) is not the prized "default" it once was in advertising schedules, it is still important in determining the weight (GRP) needed in campaigns. To estimate the coverage of a desired audience, researchers need continuous monitoring of television viewing such as that provided by the Nielsen people meter samples for the "Television Index" (national programming). From these national measures media researchers have been able to develop statistical projections for local market estimates. Because these are not direct observations, reach tables are used only as planning guides, not for schedule decisions for specific markets.

Function   For those planning spot television schedules, reach estimators give rough indications of how many GRP are needed for a desired coverage. This assists estimates for impact, for allocations of dollars between markets, and finally for campaign budgeting.

Format Notes   Use of tables, such as the one on the next page, demands certain implicit understandings. First, the monthly GRP levels should be spread somewhat evenly throughout the four-week schedule period. Should an advertiser run all commercials in one week, the reach levels indicated by the table would be overstated. Schedule dispersion is needed to optimize reach opportunities. Dispersion in programming and programming types is also necessary if the table estimates are expected to be valid.

Media planners and buyers who want maximum reach opportunities must key on the concept of "different": different stations, different types of programs, different days and parts of the day.

Finally, markets with heavy penetration of cable-connected households will not produce the reach estimation without investing in cable programming sources. With expanded choice options, cable viewers are much less likely to be found in local station programming alone.

Illustration   There are two ways to use the table. If the dollar allocation is firm the planner finds the affordable GRP level, and then estimates the affordable reach. If the reach level is the marker then the planner learns how many GRP are needed to achieve the reach. This leads to cost estimating for television.

Note that reach estimates are arranged by three programming periods. Planners know that to use the estimate column all the GRP must be scheduled in either "early news," "primetime," or "late night." This table does not estimate any combination of dayparts. If planners wanted the reach estimate for a schedule of both prime evening and early news, a model of the combined GRP would be supplied for further statistical projection. Many advertising agencies and media software vendors have the mathematical software to produce reach estimates from mixed schedules.

Estimated Adult Viewer Reach for Selected Dayparts (Spot Television Programming)

Four Week GRP	Percent Adult Viewers Exposed		
	Early News (M-S)	Primetime (M-S)	Late Night (M-F)
50	31–33	36–41	26–28
100	39–41	51–57	32–36
150	50–53	60–68	40–43
200[1]	61–64	68–74	49–52
300[1]	65–68	76–81	57–59
400[1]	69–72	81–86	63–65

[1]Must use two or more stations per market
Source: Agency Estimates

Source 22
Network Radio Reach and Frequency Estimator

Description   Radio usage is highly selective to listeners. This requires those making network radio plans to be sure that desired exposure of different listeners is accomplished. The best source for this data comes from Statistical Research, Inc. and its RADAR reports. These are national phone survey measurements completed quarterly.

From many model schedules analyzed for agencies and network sales groups, a forecast table has been created.

Function   Though radio is thought of as a "frequency" medium, planners are still concerned about maximum coverage of a target audience. When one compares the possible reach levels of network radio with those of network television, it is clear that caution should be used in building radio schedules that will provide adequate reach and frequency.

Format Notes   The reach and frequency table used is for adult men and women, the largest target for network radio. It should be noted that unlike television, there are a number of markets where network radio programming is not available. Currently, national radio can cover about three-quarters of U.S. adults (that is using all of the 30 or more radio networks).

The reach and frequency estimates shown are based on schedules that are dispersed throughout an 18-hour day (6 a.m. to midnight) and all days of the week.

The blanks on the table indicate that estimates were not made at certain GRP levels if more than one network was planned for. To illustrate, 30 GRP in a four-week period means less than 8 rating points per week. This may be a reasonable buy on one network, it is not if the ratings had to be divided between two or more networks.

Illustration   If a planner is seeking a minimum frequency of three exposures a month (3.0), there are a number of options:

One network: Must use more than 30 GRP/month
Two networks: Must divide at least 60 GRP/month
Three: Must divide at least 80 GRP/month
Four: Must divide at least 100 GRP/month

Planners checking the interaction between reach and frequency with the same GRP level need only to look at what happens at 100 GRP per month. There are four network options ranging from a 16 reach to a 34 (that's a 113 percent shift). The frequency ranges from an average of more than six messages exposed to fewer than three (2.9).

Network Radio Reach and Frequency Estimates (adult audiences and selected GRP levels)

Four-Week Total GRP	Number of Networks Used							
	One		Two		Three		Four	
	R	F	R	F	R	F	R	F
30	10	3.0	—*	—	—	—	—	—
40	11	3.6	—	—	—	—	—	—
50	12	4.2	19	2.6	—	—	—	—
60	13	4.6	20	3.0	—	—	—	—
70	14	5.0	21	3.3	—	—	—	—
80	15	5.3	22	3.6	28	2.9	—	—
90	16	5.6	23	3.9	29	3.1	—	—
100	16	6.3	25	4.0	30	3.3	34	2.9

Source: Agency estimates based on RADAR®. Statistical Research, Inc.
* Presence of "—" indicates GRP level too low for multiple net use.

Source 23
Spot Market Radio Audience Reach Estimator
....

Description   For the major MSAs (the top 50) the fragmentation of the radio audience is very high. Between AM and FM stations, and the variety of programs, listeners have much to choose from. This not only makes it hard to attain high audience reach, it makes it more difficult to estimate with strong certainty.

Media research investment tends to follow media investment in advertising. With only about 7 per cent of advertising dollars, radio does not command the significant continuous measurement needed for reach projections. But, agencies and marketers make the best of limited resources. As shown earlier, Arbitron has a diary measurement one week long for nearly 100 markets on a year-long basis. Network radio's measurement of popularity by RADAR's phone interviews adds to this picture, as do the SMRB and MRI investigations of radio listening diaries.

By careful combining of these measurements, radio analysts are able to create some statistical projections of listening patterns for monthly schedules. Note, the "cume" figures in each Arbitron local report cannot tell us how many program segments or GRP are needed to achieve the maximum reach of one station. Station cumes also do not reflect multiple station usage. Statistical projections are the only way to produce GRP to reach estimates.

Function   This is identical to spot television reach estimates. Radio reach estimates tell planners how many dollars (per market) it takes to achieve a predetermined audience reach goal. Estimators are also used to judge how much audience reach can be achieved with a fixed budget or allocation.

Format Notes   The advice given for spot television table usage goes double for spot radio. The estimates for maximum reach demand that planners and buyers use certain judgments. Multiple station purchasing is vital especially where a programming choice (e.g., music played) is provided by several stations. Using multiple dayparts is also recommended. Scheduling certain quarter hours in morning commuting periods is going to reach mostly the same commuters each day. For marketers seeking strong geographic coverage, some stations with the strongest signals should be included to ensure a broader reach base.

Illustration   The table shown here is an excerpt in that it only projects reach levels built upon the morning and evening commuting hours. Morning "drivetime" usually runs from 6 to 10 a.m. Monday through Friday. The evening commute period begins at 3 or 4 p.m. and ends at 7 or 8 p.m. Similar tables reflect midday, evening, and weekend programming.

The number of stations recommended for various GRP levels is conservative. Our advice is that you are safer using more than two stations to cover 200 monthly GRP for a 45 percent reach. If four stations could be considered then they could alternate weeks thereby balancing schedules. This type of tactic is necessary to make reach estimates simulate the real environment.

Spot Market Radio Reach Estimates for Adult Listeners (Selected Dayparts)

Monthly GRP	Percent Adults Exposed Morning and Evening Drivetime Periods
200–215[1]	45
415–430[1]	60
600–650[2]	65
825–860[2]	70

[1]Estimate based on two or more stations used.
[2]Estimate based on three or more stations used.
Source: Agency Estimates

Source 24
Daily Newspaper Multiple Issue Reach Estimator

Description   From a history of Scarborough survey data, agency media researchers have been able to create a model that estimates the increase of reach with the use of additional insertions. With this a planner can make at least a rough judgment on how additional newspaper ads will influence exposure or reader coverage.

Function   This is a generic table in that it has smoothed data from at least 50 different DMA areas. While the model does adjust for circulation differences between markets ("HH Coverage"), it is worth noting that all newspapers at a given circulation penetration were averaged for the figures shown. The accuracy to any specific market is at question, especially for markets where single copy sales are strong.

Format Notes   The "coverage" column is calculated by dividing newspaper average daily circulation in the DMA by the total homes in the DMA.

As has been true of other reach estimates, dispersion has been factored into model projections. The estimate for two insertions is based on different days and different weeks. Those planners considering consecutive day scheduling should lower the estimate.

Similarly, planners thinking about combining Saturday and Sunday editions with weekday editions should discuss this with media researchers before using these figures that are based on weekday patterns.

Illustration   If a planner was considering the effect of additional insertions in Dallas (DMA coverage of 35 percent), the table would indicate an increase of 7 percentage points in reach or an increase of 20 percent in reach.

The table reflects both male and female readership. Reach percentages are based on all the male and female adults in the DMA. Understanding this helps explain why the coverage percentage (homes) is always higher than the one-insertion reach level, which is based on adult readers rather than homes.

Daily Newspaper Adult Reader/Reach Table

Daily DMA	Reach of Adult Readers		
HH Coverage	One Insertion	Two Insertions	Four Insertions
30	27	35	43
35	32	39	52
40	36	44	57
45	39	47	62
50	42	51	63

Source: Agency Estimates

Source 25
SMRB Twelve Issue Reach and Average Frequency
....

Research Company   Simmons Market Research Bureau, Inc. (SMRB)

Description   This report, part of SMRB's publication readership research, shows how well each publication accumulates new readers on successive issues. The reach projections are carried to twelve issues, a year's worth for monthly titles, and about a calendar quarter's issues for weeklies.

The estimates are compiled from a two-stage interview of reading habits taken six to eight weeks apart. These interviews cover all types of readership: subscribers (in- and out-of-home), pass-along exposure, and professional office reading (e.g., doctor's office). The spread of time allows SMRB to measure a pattern of readership from each member of the sample. The projected readership, while based on interviews, is produced by statistical models designed to forecast exposure. In this way the twelve-issue figures are made possible.

Function   Advertisers using publication media are interested in the changes of readership over time. How many of the publication's readers see every issue? How many different people will eventually read it? How many issues of a magazine are necessary to produce a desired repeat exposure pattern (frequency)? This SMRB data helps with all these questions.

Format Notes and Illustration   The excerpt shown on the next page covers 23 of the 126 publications measured by SMRB. To explain each observation and calculation, *Rolling Stone (RS)* figures are used.

"Net Reach."   The figure shown under each of the twelve columns represents the number of readers that can be claimed by *RS*. For one issue it is 6,154,000 adults. For two issues it is 9,020,000. The difference is 2,866,000 readers who were "new" (did not see the first issue). For each issue frequency you can learn how many "new" readers were added by subtracting. The difference between issue eleven and issue twelve of *RS* is 434,000 (17,674,000 − 17,240,000). Compare this difference with the difference between issues one and two shown above.

"Rating."   As in all applications of this term, rating is a percent expression of a raw number. If 6,154,000 adults see a single issue of *Rolling Stone*, that represents 3.4 percent of all U.S. adults. To verify any of the ratings on this table divide the "net reach" figure for any of the issue columns by 182,456,000. This is the base U.S. adult population used by SMRB.

"Average Frequency."   We assume that a vast majority of a magazine's subscribers will eventually see each issue. We also know that SMRB measures nonsubscriber readership. However, nonsubscribers do not see every issue. Therefore, if an advertiser uses 5 issues of *RS* the frequency will not be 5.0. Of the total different adults seeing the 5th issue of *RS*, they, on average, will have only seen 2.31 of the five issues. The ratio is created by multiplying the single-issue audience (6,154,000) by 5 (issues). This number, 30,770,000, is the total *duplicated* reader impressions from 5 issues. However, the projected number of different readers by the fifth issue is 13,332,000. Divide the duplicated fifth issue readership by the fifth issue "net reach" and you'll find the 2.31 average frequency.

0337
M-9

THELVE ISSUE REACH AND AVERAGE FREQUENCY
TOTAL ADULT AUDIENCE
U.S. POPULATION 182,456 (IN THOUSANDS)

0337
M-9

		NUMBER OF ISSUES											
		1	2	3	4	5	6	7	8	9	10	11	12
NATURAL HISTORY	NET REACH	1306	1917	2315	2610	2845	3039	3205	3350	3478	3594	3698	3794
	AVERAGE FREQUENCY	1.00	1.36	1.69	2.00	2.30	2.58	2.85	3.12	3.38	3.64	3.89	4.13
	RATING	0.7	1.1	1.3	1.4	1.6	1.7	1.8	1.8	1.9	2.0	2.0	2.1
NEW WOMAN	NET REACH	2946	4135	4879	5419	5843	6191	6487	6744	6971	7175	7359	7527
	AVERAGE FREQUENCY	1.00	1.42	1.81	2.17	2.52	2.85	3.18	3.49	3.80	4.11	4.40	4.70
	RATING	1.6	2.3	2.7	3.0	3.2	3.4	3.6	3.7	3.8	3.9	4.0	4.1
NEW YORK	NET REACH	1714	2549	3100	3511	3838	4110	4343	4546	4726	4888	5036	5170
	AVERAGE FREQUENCY	1.00	1.34	1.66	1.95	2.23	2.50	2.76	3.02	3.26	3.51	3.74	3.98
	RATING	0.9	1.4	1.7	1.9	2.1	2.3	2.4	2.5	2.6	2.7	2.8	2.8
THE NEW YORKER	NET REACH	2576	3705	4426	4956	5374	5719	6012	6268	6494	6697	6881	7049
	AVERAGE FREQUENCY	1.00	1.39	1.75	2.08	2.40	2.70	3.00	3.29	3.57	3.85	4.12	4.38
	RATING	1.4	2.0	2.4	2.7	2.9	3.1	3.3	3.4	3.6	3.7	3.8	3.9
NEWSWEEK	NET REACH	21396	29921	35136	38854	41727	44059	46017	47700	49173	50483	51659	52727
	AVERAGE FREQUENCY	1.00	1.43	1.83	2.20	2.56	2.91	3.25	3.59	3.92	4.24	4.56	4.87
	RATING	11.7	16.4	19.3	21.3	22.9	24.1	25.2	26.1	27.0	27.7	28.3	28.9
THE N.Y. TIMES MAGAZINE	NET REACH	3859	5578	6680	7490	8130	8658	9107	9498	9844	10154	10435	10692
	AVERAGE FREQUENCY	1.00	1.38	1.73	2.06	2.37	2.67	2.97	3.25	3.53	3.80	4.07	4.33
	RATING	2.1	3.1	3.7	4.1	4.5	4.7	5.0	5.2	5.4	5.6	5.7	5.9
OMNI	NET REACH	2338	3746	4751	5531	6169	6707	7172	7583	7949	8280	8582	8859
	AVERAGE FREQUENCY	1.00	1.25	1.48	1.69	1.90	2.09	2.28	2.47	2.65	2.82	3.00	3.17
	RATING	1.3	2.1	2.6	3.0	3.4	3.7	3.9	4.2	4.4	4.5	4.7	4.9
1,001 HOME IDEAS	NET REACH	3771	5750	7087	8094	8901	9574	10150	10654	11102	11505	11870	12205
	AVERAGE FREQUENCY	1.00	1.31	1.60	1.86	2.12	2.36	2.60	2.83	3.06	3.28	3.49	3.71
	RATING	2.1	3.2	3.9	4.4	4.9	5.2	5.6	5.8	6.1	6.3	6.5	6.7
ORGANIC GARDENING	NET REACH	2544	3596	4257	4740	5118	5431	5696	5926	6130	6313	6478	6629
	AVERAGE FREQUENCY	1.00	1.41	1.79	2.15	2.49	2.81	3.13	3.43	3.74	4.03	4.32	4.61
	RATING	1.4	2.0	2.3	2.6	2.8	3.0	3.1	3.2	3.4	3.5	3.6	3.6
OUTDOOR LIFE	NET REACH	7310	10413	12369	13794	14912	15830	16609	17285	17882	18416	18899	19339
	AVERAGE FREQUENCY	1.00	1.40	1.77	2.12	2.45	2.77	3.08	3.38	3.68	3.97	4.25	4.54
	RATING	4.0	5.7	6.8	7.6	8.2	8.7	9.1	9.5	9.8	10.1	10.4	10.6
PARADE MAGAZINE	NET REACH	67853	85322	94634	100774	105268	108769	111613	113991	116025	117795	119357	120750
	AVERAGE FREQUENCY	1.00	1.59	2.15	2.69	3.22	3.74	4.26	4.76	5.26	5.76	6.25	6.74
	RATING	37.2	46.8	51.9	55.2	57.7	59.6	61.2	62.5	63.6	64.6	65.4	66.2
PARENTING	NET REACH	1947	2877	3487	3940	4300	4599	4855	5077	5275	5453	5614	5761
	AVERAGE FREQUENCY	1.00	1.35	1.68	1.98	2.26	2.54	2.81	3.07	3.32	3.57	3.82	4.06
	RATING	1.1	1.6	1.9	2.2	2.4	2.5	2.7	2.8	2.9	3.0	3.1	3.2
PARENTS	NET REACH	6643	8997	10420	11437	12228	12874	13419	13891	14307	14679	15015	15321
	AVERAGE FREQUENCY	1.00	1.48	1.91	2.32	2.72	3.10	3.47	3.83	4.18	4.53	4.87	5.20
	RATING	3.6	4.9	5.7	6.3	6.7	7.1	7.4	7.6	7.8	8.0	8.2	8.4
PEOPLE	NET REACH	28488	41531	49722	55594	60125	63787	66845	69461	71739	73752	75551	77176
	AVERAGE FREQUENCY	1.00	1.37	1.72	2.05	2.37	2.68	2.98	3.28	3.57	3.86	4.15	4.43
	RATING	15.6	22.8	27.3	30.5	33.0	35.0	36.6	38.1	39.3	40.4	41.4	42.3
PLAYBOY	NET REACH	8337	11528	13488	14897	15995	16893	17653	18311	18890	19408	19875	20302
	AVERAGE FREQUENCY	1.00	1.45	1.85	2.24	2.61	2.96	3.31	3.64	3.97	4.30	4.61	4.93
	RATING	4.6	6.3	7.4	8.2	8.8	9.3	9.7	10.0	10.4	10.6	10.9	11.1
POPULAR MECHANICS	NET REACH	5655	7889	9274	10276	11060	11702	12247	12719	13136	13509	13846	14154
	AVERAGE FREQUENCY	1.00	1.43	1.83	2.20	2.56	2.90	3.23	3.56	3.87	4.19	4.49	4.79
	RATING	3.1	4.3	5.1	5.6	6.1	6.4	6.7	7.0	7.2	7.4	7.6	7.8
POPULAR SCIENCE	NET REACH	4555	6774	8234	9319	10182	10898	11509	12041	12513	12937	13321	13672
	AVERAGE FREQUENCY	1.00	1.35	1.66	1.96	2.24	2.51	2.77	3.03	3.28	3.52	3.76	4.00
	RATING	2.5	3.7	4.5	5.1	5.6	6.0	6.3	6.6	6.9	7.1	7.3	7.5
PRACTICAL HOMEOWNER	NET REACH	1281	1834	2186	2444	2648	2816	2959	3084	3194	3293	3383	3465
	AVERAGE FREQUENCY	1.00	1.40	1.76	2.10	2.42	2.73	3.03	3.32	3.61	3.89	4.17	4.44
	RATING	0.7	1.0	1.2	1.3	1.5	1.5	1.6	1.7	1.8	1.8	1.9	1.9
PREVENTION	NET REACH	6154	8657	10219	11352	12239	12968	13585	14121	14594	15017	15400	15749
	AVERAGE FREQUENCY	1.00	1.42	1.81	2.17	2.51	2.85	3.17	3.49	3.80	4.10	4.40	4.69
	RATING	3.4	4.7	5.6	6.2	6.7	7.1	7.4	7.7	8.0	8.2	8.4	8.6
READER'S DIGEST	NET REACH	36930	47627	53681	57844	60991	63508	65597	67379	68928	70297	71522	72629
	AVERAGE FREQUENCY	1.00	1.55	2.06	2.55	3.03	3.49	3.94	4.38	4.82	5.25	5.68	6.10
	RATING	20.2	26.1	29.4	31.7	33.4	34.8	36.0	36.9	37.8	38.5	39.2	39.8
REDBOOK	NET REACH	10534	14516	16949	18694	20051	21159	22095	22903	23615	24251	24825	25347
	AVERAGE FREQUENCY	1.00	1.45	1.86	2.25	2.63	2.99	3.34	3.68	4.02	4.34	4.67	4.99
	RATING	5.8	8.0	9.3	10.2	11.0	11.6	12.1	12.6	12.9	13.3	13.6	13.9
ROAD & TRACK	NET REACH	3838	5254	6118	6740	7225	7622	7959	8251	8508	8738	8946	9136
	AVERAGE FREQUENCY	1.00	1.46	1.88	2.28	2.66	3.02	3.38	3.72	4.06	4.39	4.72	5.04
	RATING	2.1	2.9	3.4	3.7	4.0	4.2	4.4	4.5	4.7	4.8	4.9	5.0
ROLLING STONE	NET REACH	6154	9020	10878	12248	13332	14227	14989	15652	16238	16764	17240	17674
	AVERAGE FREQUENCY	1.00	1.36	1.70	2.01	2.31	2.60	2.87	3.15	3.41	3.67	3.93	4.18
	RATING	3.4	4.9	6.0	6.7	7.3	7.8	8.2	8.6	8.9	9.2	9.4	9.7

Source 26
SMRB Duplication of Average Issue Audiences
....

Research Company   Simmons Market Research Bureau, Inc. (SMRB)

Description   This report by SMRB shows the audience interaction of all measured magazines in pair combinations (the overlap of readers between two magazines).

People who regularly read magazines read more than one. It follows then that the field interviews will learn these combinations from each sample member.

The duplication analyses are called *between* measures, while Source 25 covers *within* measures (duplicated readership of a single publication). Together, these reports give us insight as to the dynamic nature of magazine reading habits.

Function   Media plans calling for magazines and other publications usually include a combination of print activity. Selection of titles will take into consideration the combination of readers. In some situations a high degree of overlap will be desired; duplication supports frequency needs. In other circumstances, the media planner wants strong unduplication to support reach needs. Either way this data is critical to schedule development.

As for larger combinations (more than two publications) media planners may derive estimates (probability models) by using SMRB's pair data.

Format Notes   "**Net Unduplicated.**"   This means the number of readers that read only one of the paired magazines.

"**Duplicated.**"   This means the number of readers that read both of the paired magazines.

"**Single Issue Aud.**"   This represents the total readership of one magazine and one issue of the magazine.

"**Two Issue Net Aud.**"   This represents the number of *different* readers exposed after two issues of one magazine. It is an excerpt of the "within" measurement we found in Source 25.

Note: The excerpt shown lists a number of magazine "groups." These are collections of magazines owned by the same publisher (e.g., Hearst or Hachette) and sold as a group to advertisers. In such cases you are not dealing with a "pair" of magazines in the data shown.

Illustration   A reasonable example will show how these data can be used. The audience is adults 18 to 49 years. Planners for a male-oriented product would probably consider sport magazines such as *Sports Illustrated* (SI) and *Golf* as a possible pair.

"**Finding Gross Combined Readership.**"   This means adding the individual audiences of the two magazines. The figure for *SI* is at the top of its column listing (17,479,000). The figure for *Golf* is just to the right of the title listing (3,008,000). Together they have a combined readership of 20,487,000 (17,479 + 3,008).

"**Finding Net (Unduplicated) Readership.**"   The first section of data is titled "Net Unduplicated," and it is here that the pair figure is shown. The figure is in the intersect of the two titles. Go across from *Golf* until you are under *SI*. The number shown, 18,733,000 (zeros added) is the answer. These are different adults covered by the two titles.

"Finding Duplicated Readership." The lower section of the page covers the overlapped audiences. The intersect shows the figure 947. This means, of the combined readership of the two magazines, 947,000 read both *Golf* and *SI*.

"Finding the Audience Reach (%)." What percentage of the adult 18–49 audience is covered by the two? Find the unduplicated figure (18,733,000) and divide it by the total U.S. adults 18–49 (120,585,000). It is listed at the top lefthand corner of the page. The answer is 15.5 percent. A single issue of both magazines will cover that percentage.

To select the combination that best serves the firm's needs, various pairs of sport or male-oriented magazines would be compared before the selections are made.

0062 H-4 PAGE 22				DUPLICATION OF AVERAGE ISSUE AUDIENCES							0062 H-4 PAGE 22

AGE: 18-49 / ADULTS

ROWS - FIELD & STREAM TO LADIES' HOME JOURNAL (IN THOUSANDS) COLUMNS - SMITHSONIAN TO SUNSET

	U.S.TOTAL	SMITH-SONIAN	SOAP OPERA DIGEST	SOUTHERN LIVING	SPORT	THE SPORTING NEWS	SPORTS AFIELD	SPORTS ILLUS-TRATED	STAR	SUNDAY MAGAZINE NETWORK	SUNSET
SINGLE ISSUE AUD.	120585	3956	5439	4238	2678	2801	2566	17479	8267	23901	2091
COVERAGE	100.0	3.2	4.5	3.5	2.2	2.3	2.1	14.4	6.8	19.8	1.7
TWO ISSUE NET AUD.	120585	5707	7651	5773	3922	4011	3817	23606	11503	30030	2807
COVERAGE	100.0	4.7	6.3	4.7	3.2	3.3	3.1	19.5	9.5	24.9	2.3

NET UNDUPLICATED

	U.S.TOTAL	SMITH-SONIAN	SOAP OPERA DIGEST	SOUTHERN LIVING	SPORT	THE SPORTING NEWS	SPORTS AFIELD	SPORTS ILLUS-TRATED	STAR	SUNDAY MAGAZINE NETWORK	SUNSET
FIELD & STREAM	10567	11088	12661	11189	9724	9806	8925	23032	15118	30073	9434
FINANCIAL WORLD	1455	4935	6461	5206	3668	3813	3547	18243	9270	24558	3118
FIRST FOR WOMEN	5833	7981	8800	7911	6805	6915	6682	21320	11741	27143	6203
FOOD & WINE	1973	5220	6760	5428	4002	4143	3940	18583	9525	24810	3437
FORBES	3241	5923	7626	6250	4786	4898	4714	19020	10387	25354	4249
FORTUNE	4208	6527	8277	6928	5415	5546	5364	19415	10957	25816	4914
GQ/GENTLEMEN'S QUARTERLY	5523	7446	9033	7866	6161	6251	6291	19823	11673	26809	5818
GLAMOUR	10196	10582	11413	10602	9485	9618	9399	23786	14009	29300	8762
GOLF	3008	6005	7578	6320	4633	4711	4615	18733	10315	25555	4238
GOLF DIGEST	3538	6426	8015	6745	4988	5113	5008	18954	10745	25963	4622
GOLF DIGEST/TENNIS (NET)	5114	7545	9178	7846	6114	6174	6195	19820	11877	26952	5768
GOOD HOUSEKEEPING	17593	16183	16879	15843	15291	15348	15121	29126	19284	33736	14429
GOURMET	2735	5664	7315	5962	4554	4686	4486	19063	9969	25166	3898
HACHETTE MAG.NETWRK(NET)	18989	17622	19517	18089	16315	16399	16471	27734	21580	34971	16238
HACHETTE MTRCYC GRP(NET)	4176	6783	8399	7175	5552	5637	5388	19570	11071	26396	5104
HARPER'S BAZAAR	3255	5949	7304	6190	4805	4947	4695	19347	10143	25404	4200
HEALTH	2783	5631	7058	5836	4327	4499	4266	18878	9779	25178	3772
HEARST GOLD BUY (NET)	12559	12097	13603	12139	11017	11232	11076	24466	16062	30184	10574
HEARST HOME BUY (NET)	11369	11692	13173	11280	10829	10879	10565	24785	15780	30352	10062
HEARST MAN POWER (NET)	11256	11530	13282	11767	10126	10305	8606	22811	15647	30214	9986
HEARST WOMAN POWER (NET)	34628	30088	30062	29389	29616	29637	29281	42028	32109	44909	28646
HOME	3330	6063	7447	6157	4788	4963	4708	19366	10198	25584	4167
HOME MECHANIX	2110	5388	6894	5619	4119	4236	4013	18578	9612	25126	3564
HOMEOWNER	2304	5412	6843	5639	4133	4287	4016	18714	9583	25155	3565
HG/HOUSE & GARDEN	2380	5376	6853	5536	4254	4359	4139	18876	9593	25042	3604
HOUSE BEAUTIFUL	3785	6345	7790	6456	5194	5273	5114	19724	10532	25854	4533
INC.	1714	4923	6504	5253	3713	3824	3639	18328	9302	24635	3145
INSIDE SPORTS	4968	7237	8809	7568	5381	5712	5749	18931	11398	26462	5532
JET	9229	11123	11934	11236	9705	9805	9795	23247	14338	29715	9322
LADIES' HOME JOURNAL	13330	12958	13658	12578	11928	12014	11838	25979	16060	31042	11159

DUPLICATED

	U.S.TOTAL	SMITH-SONIAN	SOAP OPERA DIGEST	SOUTHERN LIVING	SPORT	THE SPORTING NEWS	SPORTS AFIELD	SPORTS ILLUS-TRATED	STAR	SUNDAY MAGAZINE NETWORK	SUNSET
FIELD & STREAM	4281	292	203	474	378	420	1066	1871	574	1253	82
FINANCIAL WORLD	640	68	27	80	58	36	67	284	45	390	22
FIRST FOR WOMEN	2485	134	798	486	32	44	43	317	685	916	47
FOOD & WINE	837	141	84	215	81	63	32	300	147	496	59
FORBES	1194	250	31	205	109	120	70	676	97	764	60
FORTUNE	1586	326	59	207	160	152	100	960	207	982	74
GQ/GENTLEMEN'S QUARTERLY	2071	307	203	169	314	347	72	1452	392	889	70
GLAMOUR	3564	254	906	516	73	63	48	573	1139	1481	210
GOLF	1394	152	62	119	246	291	152	947	154	546	54
GOLF DIGEST	1688	143	37	106	302	300	172	1137	135	551	82
GOLF DIGEST/TENNIS (NET)	2515	225	76	206	379	442	187	1473	205	764	138
GOOD HOUSEKEEPING	7998	569	1356	1190	183	249	241	1148	1778	2960	458
GOURMET	1161	240	72	225	72	63	28	364	247	683	141
HACHETTE MAG.NETWRK(NET)	10048	852	441	668	881	921	614	4263	1206	3449	372
HACHETTE MTRCYC GRP(NET)	1873	197	65	87	150	188	203	932	220	529	11
HARPER'S BAZAAR	1075	172	301	213	38	19	37	297	289	662	56
HEALTH	722	77	134	154	103	55	53	353	240	476	72
HEARST GOLD BUY (NET)	4931	603	582	844	406	314	235	1757	951	2461	263
HEARST HOME BUY (NET)	5198	548	549	1241	132	206	285	977	771	1833	313
HEARST MAN POWER (NET)	4764	436	167	480	561	506	1970	2678	630	1697	115
HEARST WOMAN POWER (NET)	19940	1152	2661	2133	346	448	569	2735	3442	6276	729
HOME	1065	91	190	278	87	36	56	310	267	515	123
HOME MECHANIX	914	79	58	130	71	77	65	412	168	287	39
HOMEOWNER	745	68	121	123	69	38	75	289	209	270	51
HG/HOUSE & GARDEN	798	169	175	291	13	31	16	192	263	448	77
HOUSE BEAUTIFUL	1346	176	215	347	49	93	18	320	301	612	124
INC.	455	117	20	70	50	61	12	235	50	351	31
INSIDE SPORTS	1939	172	84	123	750	542	271	2001	322	893	13
JET	5377	136	808	304	276	300	75	1535	1232	1489	73
LADIES' HOME JOURNAL	5386	356	1139	1018	108	145	87	857	1566	2217	291

Source 27
Outdoor Posters: Adult Reach Estimator
....

Description   Exposure to outdoor advertising is as different to measure as any other mass medium. No professionals question the potential for coverage because our use of the automobile is unquestioned. The problem relates to validating that motorists and passengers make visual contact with the message. It is doubtful that measurement technology will ever monitor this accurately.

In lieu of direct observation the outdoor industry, in conjunction with advertising professionals, uses a three-element process to make reach estimates. First the street, road, or highway must be measured for traffic density. Outdoor calls this daily effective circulation (DEC). Then, some estimate of persons per vehicle must be agreed upon. SMRB has estimated an adult vehicle load factor of 1.35 adults (age 18 and over), and the Traffic Audit Bureau (TAB) has found this acceptable (the previous factor was 1.75). The third element is a visibility standard that rates a location's ability to be noticed from passing vehicles.

Function   Ideally, each market area should have adult reach levels directly linked to the GRP needed. These are available for individual plans; however, more generic estimates (such as the one included here) satisfy the needs of preliminary evaluation.

Format Notes   "GRP."   The outdoor companies are most comfortable in estimating the rating points generated from each location. The package of locations offered to advertisers is designed in this manner. The "daily" designation is somewhat misleading in that estimates often mirror the commuter week of five days, and not seven.

"Daily/Monthly Adult Reach."   The daily estimates are included for reference purposes only. Many motorists do not travel on identical routes every day. By the end of 30 days, however, the opportunity for exposure is pretty sure.

Estimated Unduplicated Exposure of Adults to Daily and Monthly Outdoor Activity

| | Percentage of Adults Reached | |
GRP Per Day	Daily	Monthly
50	15–20	80–85
100	25–35	87–92

Based on T.A.B. and SMRB data

S·E·C·T·I·O·N T·W·O

Exercises

The only way to become familiar and comfortable with a source is to practice with it. Explanations help, but are no substitute for experience in using a source.

Working with each of these sources using the exercises in this section has a two-fold benefit. First, it demonstrates the capabilities of the source by illustrating the sorts of inquiries that can be answered. Then, working with the information generated using a step process, you will better understand how it contributes to problem-solving.

Once you have mastered the individual source, you will want to investigate those sources that can be used in combination (for example, cost and rating estimators).

Exercise 1

. . . .

Reference   Mediamark Research Inc. (MRI) Marketing Data (Source 1)

Questions   1. Which consumption level dominates regular cola use by adult women? Are there more heavy, medium, or light drinkers?

2. The illustration showed that we were most likely to find a heavy consumer of cola between the ages of 18 and 24 years. At what age are we most likely to find a "light" drinker?

3. Which census region holds the most drinkers of regular cola? Should this be surprising to "Coke" or "Pepsi" managers? Why or why not?

4. Describe the relationship between household income and heavy cola usage. Write a single sentence that summarizes without quoting any numbers.

Exercise 2

. . . .

Reference   *Survey of Buying Power* (Source 2)

Questions   1. Which metro area in New Mexico has the highest percentage of adults 18 to 34 years old?

2. What percentage of the *city* of Santa Fe's households have EBI of $50,000 and over?

3. Which metro area in New Mexico has the highest Buying Power Index?

4. How much did Albuquerque spend in food stores? What did the average household spend?

Exercise 3

. . . .

Reference   *Editor and Publisher Market Guide* (Source 3)

Questions   1. Which shopping center listed in Minneapolis has the largest number of stores? Is it really larger than the Mall of America? (Note: you will need another reference to answer the last question.)

2. Is there a K-Mart in New Ulm?

3. How many railroads serve Owatonna?

4. Which of the discount chains has the most outlets in Minneapolis?

5. If your firm distributed water softening systems, how would you appraise New Ulm's market potential?

Exercise 4

. . . .

Reference   LNA/MediaWatch Multi-Media Service (Source 4)

Questions   1. How much did the "Victoria Palace Theater" spend in spot television? When were these dollars spent (name the potential months)?

2. What percent of the spending for the "Walter Kerr Theater" was done in magazine for the first quarter of 1995?

3. When the listing shows both "94" and "95" "YTD" (year-to-date), what is being compared?

4. Based on this excerpt page alone, which medium has the most investment (total dollars) for 95 YTD? Which medium had the most advertisers?

Exercise 5

· ·

Reference   LNA Newspaper Spending (Source 5)

Questions   1. How much has "Home Improvement Specialists" spent during the first six months of 1995? Was its spending balanced between the first two quarters?

2. Which of the firms shown appears to be the most widespread nationally? How many metro areas does its newspaper spending cover?

3. For the firm known as "Kelly Window & Door Contractors," which newspaper received most of its advertising dollars? In what state is that newspaper located?

Exercise 6

· ·

Reference   Nielsen Ratings Audience Estimates (Source 6)

Questions   1. Which program has the highest average HHLD Audience rating?

2. Which program accumulated the largest household audience for its duration? This is the "TA%."

3. "Roseanne" has the highest share of audience for any of the quarter-hours shown, followed closely by two shows, "Ellen" and "Primetime Live." How can the latter two programs both have 23 shares when their ratings are different (e.g., 14.7 and 13.3)? Hint: you do not have to make any calculations to answer this question.

Exercise 7
. . . .

Reference   Nielsen Ratings Audience Estimates for Local Market Television Programming (Source 7)

Questions   Use the 2:00 to 2:30 p.m. segment shown in Source 7 to answer these questions.

1. What was the share of the most popular program?

2. With which audience segment (age/gender) was KDAF's Saturday Movie most popular?

3. Which station has the best chance to deliver the largest male audience between 18 and 34 years? Does program consistency influence your choice?

4. Which station shows the most steady share trend? By steady, we mean having the least amount of fluctuation.

Exercise 8
. . . .

Reference   Arbitron Radio Local Market Reports

Situation   As a radio buyer for a small chain of music stores (CDs) located in metro San Francisco, answer these questions about the stations shown in the Arbitron excerpt in Source 8.

1. Identify the top three stations during weekday evenings based on average quarter-hour estimates.

2. What is the combined share of these stations?

3. Using the same daypart, how many weekly GRP would you have if you bought 20 announcements on KBLX-FM and the same number on KABL-FM?

4. How many total target impressions would you have for a 10-week schedule using the stations noted in Question 3?

5. How many announcements would you have to buy on KABL to equal one announcement bought on KABL-FM? Use the 10 a.m. to 3 p.m. daypart.

Exercise 9

. . . .

Reference   SMRB Demographic Status of Adult Magazine Readers (Source 9)

Questions   1. How many adult females read *Self* magazine?

2. Which magazine has the highest percentage of its readership in the heading "Principal Shoppers?"

3. In which publication are you most likely to find a male reader? In which publication do you find the most male readers? Why aren't these two answers identical?

4. If your client's target audiences followed closely U.S. demographics by gender, name three publications that would have your serious consideration. Explain.

5. How many adult GRP would you have from one issue of *Newsweek*, *Reader's Digest*, and *Parade Magazine*?

Exercise 10

. . . .

Reference   Newspaper Circulation Analysis by DMA Area (Source 10)

Questions   1. What is the fewest number of newspapers needed for a DMA penetration of 45 percent on a daily basis? Base your figure on the most popular newspapers in the DMA.

2. What is the combined circulation of *Time* and *Newsweek* in the DMA?

3. If the *Victoria Advocate* has a DMA circulation of 8,840, why isn't that the figure listed under the heading "20% MAC Daily"?

4. Explain why this source cannot answer this question: what is the unduplicated penetration of *Time* and *Newsweek* in the Houston DMA?

Exercise 11

• •

Reference   Network Television 30-Second Participation Cost Estimation (Source 11)

Questions   1. Based on the highest cost factor, how much would 250 GRP cost in *Evening News* if the schedule equally covered the second and third quarters?

2. For a fourth quarter purchase, what is the most daytime GRP obtainable for $750,000. What is the fewest day GRP a buyer should expect to obtain?

3. Using highest prices, how much allocation could be saved if all the late-evening positions ran in the first quarter instead of the fourth quarter? The allocation is based on 125 GRP.

4. A company is considering negotiating schedules in which half the GRP would be in early news and half would be in late evening. Using the highest CPR rates on a yearly average, how many GRP in each of the dayparts could be affordable for $2,500,000?

Exercise 12

• •

Reference   Cable Network Television 30-Second Cost Estimator (Nighttime) (Source 12)

Questions   1. Before any estimating can be done, a single unit price must be determined. For the prime evening period prepare a composite unit cost individually for each of these networks: A&E, USA, and Nick at Nite. The composite is as follows: two-thirds of the highest price plus one-third of the lowest prime price. What are the operating prices for these networks?

2. How much would it cost for 120 units for USA and 45 units on Nick at Nite? Show them separately and combined.

3. How many units can we expect from $950,000 if we split those dollars evenly between A&E and USA?

4. If Nielsen reported an average target rating of .3 (that's three tenths of one point), how many GRP could we expect from the USA portion of Question 2?

Exercise 13

. . . .

Reference   Spot Television 30-Second Participation Cost Estimator (Source 13)

Questions   1. How much would 200 daytime GRP cost in both Denver and Phoenix if both markets were scheduled in the second quarter?

2. How much more would the plan in question 1 cost if you substituted the fourth quarter for the second?

3. There is $25,000 allocated for early news schedules to cover both New Orleans and Memphis DMAs. If both schedules were run in the second quarter, how many GRP could we expect? Assume that each market should receive the same number of GRP.

4. How much would the total savings be if a prime time schedule for the ''top 10'' markets (300 GRP per market) was shifted from the fourth quarter to the second quarter?

5. Based on the plan shown in question 3, how many more GRP could be expected if half the GRP were in early news and half were in daytime? Each market is to be treated equally.

Exercise 14

. . . .

Reference   Network Radio 30-Second Announcement Cost Estimators (Source 14)

Questions   1. For an adult female audience, how many network GRP could be purchased for $925,000 if the GRP were split evenly between mornings and afternoon drive times?

2. The budget for network radio is $1,700,000. If the schedules were split evenly between Rush Limbaugh and CNN + , how many total commercials could be purchased?

3. If the average rating for the network you are negotiating with for a Monday to Friday afternoon drive schedule is 0.9, how many weeks can be purchased (at 35 GRP per week) for $2,400,000?

4. How much will it cost (in morning drive rates) to reach an audience of adult women if you want 75 GRP per week for 13 weeks?

Exercise 15

• •

Reference   Spot Market Radio Cost Estimators (30-Second Units) (Source 15)

Questions   1. The budget allocation is $875,000. The target audience is women 18 to 34. How many GRP can we get from the top 40 markets? At a minimum of 100 GRP per week, how long could the flight last (in weeks)?

2. For men 25 to 54 the cost per rating point for a special ESPN package is $2,700. How many spot markets, beginning with New York, could be bought for the same price?

3. The plan calls for 150 adult female GRP for each market per week. How much will a 12-week schedule cost for the top 30 markets?

4. The target audience is adult males. The market priorities (in order of importance) are Boston, Dallas, and then Seattle. The GRP minimum is 400 for a month-long campaign. The allocation is $140,000. Can all three markets fit under the cost cap?

Exercise 16

• •

Reference   Major Market Daily Newspaper Cost Estimator (Source 16)

Questions   1. What would the total cost be for a 4-column 10-inch ad run three times in Detroit, Boston, Houston, and Chicago?

2. For a budget of $1,650,000, can 1,000 column inches be scheduled in each of these markets: New York, Dallas, Philadelphia, and Boston? Show the calculations for each market as well as the total.

3. For a schedule of 1800 column inches in each market, which market areas can be included for an allocation of $2,700,000? Work your calculations in descending order by size (begin with New York City).

4. Based on the SAU rates we know that for the same dollars we can buy more inches in Philadelphia than we can in Detroit. The ad unit is, however, 3 columns by 14 inches in depth. For an allocation of $97,000 how many more ad units can we buy in Philadelphia than in Detroit?

Exercise 17

....

Reference   SRDS Daily Newspaper Rates and Information (Source 17)

Questions

1. What is the price of one (weekday) ad unit measuring 4 columns by 13 inches?

2. How many weekday units are affordable if each unit is 2 columns by 7 inches and the market budget is $47,000?

3. The firm plans to use 1,875 column inches on the contract. What are the correct rates to use for weekday or Sunday insertions?

4. For a black and white 3-color unit, what would be a Sunday cost using the applicable rate from 1,875 inches?

Exercise 18

....

Reference   SRDS Magazine Rates and Information (Source 18)

Questions

1. What is the correct price for each of ten 1-page units?

2. If you used six 1/3-page ads and three 2/3-page ads in a year, what would the correct price be for each size? What would the total cost be for the whole schedule?

3. If you could take advantage of the 18-page "Bulk Discounts," what would the correct price be for each page 4-color ad?

Exercise 19

• •

Reference   SRDS Spot Television Rates and Information (Source 19)

Questions   1. For daytime ("9–noon") rotation, how many P-4 units could you buy if you can afford four 30-second spots at a P-1 price?

2. Using the prime time daypart, what is the range of prices in the P-2 price category?

3. What will it cost for five 30-second announcements per week in the "Tonight Show" if the station will accept three at P-3 and two at P-4 prices?

Exercise 20

• •

Reference   Market Cost Estimator for Thirty-Sheet Outdoor Billboards (Source 20)

Questions   1. What is the monthly cost for these three markets: New York, Philadelphia, and Washington, D.C.?

2. If you needed a three-month schedule, which metro areas could you cover with a total dollar allocation of $3.6 million? Work your calculation from the top down (begin with New York).

3. The creative production manager needs to estimate paper needs for a schedule of the top five metro markets. What are the total estimated posters needed per month?

Exercise 21

· ·

Reference   Spot Market Television Audience Reach Estimators (Source 21)

Questions   1. If the cost of a rating point was the same for all dayparts, which daypart is the most effective for reach?

2. If the typical early news program in the market had an adult rating of 12.0, how many programs would you use to achieve a 50 percent adult reach in four weeks?

3. Approximately how many prime evening GRP are necessary for a 70 percent adult reach?

4. What reach would you estimate if two late-evening programs were used (competing stations), each delivering about 25 GRP per week for four weeks?

Exercise 22

· ·

Reference   Reach and Frequency Estimations for Network Radio Schedules (Source 22)

Questions   1. If your target reach is above 30 percent of adults, what is the one option listed on the table? Can you think of another option that is not listed on this table?

2. If the planner can afford 80 GRP per month, how many networks should be planned if a goal is to have an average frequency of at least one message *per week*?

3. Look at the reach levels for one network. Explain why adding more rating points beyond 60 per month does very little to increase the reach.

4. A planner has a two-network buy with an average rating per commercial of 1.0. If the buy is for a total of 80 GRP in the four-week period, how many commercials will run on each network per week if the GRP are evenly divided between the two?

Exercise 23

. . . .

Reference   Spot Market Radio Audience Reach Estimator (Source 23)

Questions   1. If you wanted a reach of 65 from three stations, what would the weekly GRP be for each station if they shared the desired rating points equally?

2. The average drive time ratings for the stations you are considering is 1.5 per quarter-hour. For a reach of 60, how many announcements per week would have to be purchased? Your answer should indicate the minimum announcements necessary.

3. Your schedule for the month is as follows: Weeks 1 and 3 (115 GRP per week); Weeks 2 and 4 (95 GRP per week). All announcements are running in drive times. What is the estimated adult reach?

4. Lay out the scheduling pattern you would use to gain a 45 reach using three stations. Show the GRP used per station per week.

Exercise 24

. . . .

Reference   Daily Newspaper Multiple Issue Reach Estimations (Source 24)

Questions   1. At a 50 coverage level, how much increase is found between two and four insertions in a month?

2. Why is the increase in reach greater between two and four insertions than it is between one and two?

3. Why, according to the table, do newspapers with a 30 percent coverage figure cover less than 30 percent of adults with one insertion?

Exercise 25

. . . .

Reference   SMRB Adult Reach Projections (Source 25)

Questions   1. For *Newsweek*, how many new readers are added if we buy four issues instead of two issues?

2. What percentage of adults will be exposed by six issues of *Parents* magazines?

3. What is the adult GRP for six issues of *Parents*?

4. At the end of six issues of the *New Yorker*, how many has the average reader seen?

5. If we used six issues of the *New Yorker*, how many gross reader impressions would we accumulate?

Exercise 26

. . . .

Reference   SMRB Magazine Pairs Unduplicated/Duplicated Readership (Source 26)

Questions   Answer the following questions using these paired magazines: *Ladies Home Journal* and *Southern Living*.

1. What is the total combined readership of the pair? Write out the complete number with appropriate zeros.

2. *Southern Living* delivers 3.5 audience rating points per issue. What is the figure for *Ladies Home Journal*? Hint: you'll have to calculate this answer. What are the combined GRP of the two?

3. What are the combined "net unduplicated" and "duplicated" audiences for the pair?

4. What is the reach (in percent) of the pair?

Exercise 27

. . . .

Reference   Outdoor Posters: Adult Reach Estimator (Source 27)

Questions

1. If you had enough outdoor locations to give you a 100 GRP value, how many GRP would you have for a monthly contract (figure 30 days per month)?

2. If the estimated reach for a monthly program that delivered 50 GRP per day was 80, what would the average frequency of exposure be? Remember, GRP divided by reach equals average frequency.

3. This question is based upon Question 2. If you estimated there were four weeks in the month, how many exposures would the average adult driver or passenger see in a week?

A·P·P·E·N·D·I·X

Media Calculation Guide*

Print Readers per Copy

Print readers per copy is the average number of different readers who will come into contact with an average issue of a newspaper or magazine. The figure indicates the relation between circulation and the size of the reading audience. It tells how heavily each copy of the publication is used.

Needed:

    A. The average number of readers of a typical issue of the publication.

    B. The average paid circulation (number of copies).

Formula:

$$\text{Readers per copy (RPC)} = \frac{\text{Number of readers of an average issue}}{\text{Circulation of an average issue}}$$

Steps to work the formula:

1. Find the average number of readers.
2. Divide by the average circulation.

Example:

Magazine M has an average paid circulation of 1,250,000 copies, with an average readership of 3,380,000 readers per issue. How many readers per copy does this magazine have?

$$\frac{3,380,000}{1,250,000} = 2.7 \text{ readers per copy}$$

Cost per Thousand (CPM)

Cost per thousand represents the relationship between the size of a media vehicle's audience (measured as households, adults, teens, etc.) and its cost in time or space. It is used to compare the cost efficiency of one vehicle with another; for example, one magazine with another or one radio station with another. The purpose is to gain the largest audience at the lowest cost. The cost is calculated *per thousand* to provide workable dollars-and-cents figures that are easier to compare.

*These formulas provide approaches to calculating some of the basic media statistics used in advertising.

Needed:

A. Gross impressions, that is, the number of households or persons exposed to a vehicle. (If the figures are given in GRPs, convert to numerical values by multiplying GRPs by the population base.)

B. The cost of a single unit of advertising space or time. (Production costs are not normally included.)

Formula:

$$\text{Cost per thousand} = \frac{\text{Cost of media vehicle unit}}{\text{Gross audience impressions}} \times 1,000$$

Steps to work the formula:

1. Determine the number of gross impressions, households, or persons.
2. Divide the media unit cost by the number of gross impressions. This will give the cost per impression.
3. Multiply by 1,000 to convert to cost-per-thousand impressions.

Example:

A 30-second commercial on station WSSS costs $850. The Anytown rating figures for WSSS indicate 58,000 adult women viewing at that time. What is the cost per thousand adult females?

$$\frac{\$850}{58,000} \times 1,000 = \$14.65 \text{ CPM}$$

An advertiser would pay $14.65 for each 1,000 female viewers on WSSS. This figure is commonly compared with the CPM at another station to determine which one is more economical.

Broadcast Rating

A broadcast rating is the percentage of a market's population (measured as households, adults, men, women, etc.) tuned in to a specific program, station, or network at a given time. The figure is given in percent.

Needed:

A. Number of people tuned to program.

B. Total size of the audience group.

Formula:

$$\text{Rating} = \frac{\text{Audience tuned to program}}{\text{Total audience population}} \times 100$$

Steps to work the formula:

1. From research sources, find the number of estimated viewers or listeners in the audience.
2. Divide the audience figure by the total possible television set ownership population of that audience.
3. Multiply by 100 to convert to percent.

Example:

Anytown has 625,000 persons in its broadcast area. An audience survey reports that a certain program has an audience of 110,000. What is the rating for the program?

$$\frac{110,000}{625,000} \times 100 = 17.6\% \text{ rating}$$

Broadcast Share of Audience

Broadcast share of audience is the percentage of all viewers or listeners who are tuned to a particular program, station, or network at a given time. The figure is calculated in percent.

Share of audience measures the audience size as a portion of those who are in the audience of *all* stations or programs at that time, whereas the rating is a measure of that audience as a portion of all who *could be* in the audience including those who are not viewing or listening at that particular time.

Needed:

A. The number or receiving sets, households, or persons tuned to a particular program.
B. The total number of sets, households, or persons tuned in to *all* stations at the time.

Formula:

$$\text{Share of audience} = \frac{\text{Program audience size}}{\text{Total audience at the time}} \times 100$$

Steps to work the formula:

1. From a research source, determine the estimated number of viewers or listeners for the program, station, or network in question.
2. From a research source, determine the total estimated number of viewers or listeners that are the combined audiences from all programs on at that time.
3. Divide the program audience by the total audience.
4. Multiply by 100 to convert to percent.

Example:

The Anytown radio audience figures look like this at noon Monday:

Station	Number of Listeners
A	1,200
B	1,500
C	1,400
	4,100

What is the share of audience for Station B?

$$\frac{1,500}{4,100} \times 100 = 36.6\% \text{ share}$$

Radio Cumulative Rating (Cume)

The radio cumulative rating is the percentage of different persons or households hearing a certain daypart segment during the week. It indicates the potential size of a station's audience during a week's time. It is also used to measure the total reach (unduplicated listenership). *Cume* is a slang broadcast advertising term for "cumulative audience."

Note that this is a measure of potential only, dependent on continuity in the advertising. To expose all of the audience in the cumulative rating, an advertiser would need to schedule a commercial announcement during every quarter-hour of the time period for the entire week.

Needed:

    A. The total number of different listeners hearing a daypart segment on a Monday-through-Friday or a Monday-through-Sunday basis.

    B. The total number of possible listeners in the station's broadcast survey area.

Formula:

$$\text{Cumulative rating} = \frac{\text{Unduplicated listenership by daypart}}{\text{Total population of listener area}} \times 100$$

Steps to work the formula:

1. From a rating report, determine the daypart cumulative audience size.
2. Divide the audience figure by the total population of the particular audience segment.
3. Multiply by 100 to convert to percent.

Example:

Station WZYX in Anytown has a cumulative audience of 6,400 unduplicated adult listeners tuning in at least once between Monday and Sunday at 6:00 a.m.–10:00 a.m. If there are 33,000 adults in the Anytown survey area, what is the station's cumulative rating for that time period?

$$\frac{6,400}{33,000} \times 100 = 19.4\% \text{ cume}$$

Gross Rating Points (GRPs)

A gross rating point is a way to express the accumulated audience impressions developed by using a series of advertisements. A typical example might include the combined audiences from a series of magazine insertions, a package of television announcements, and an outdoor posting schedule.

GRPs are basically the sum of the ratings; that is, add the ratings for a certain time period (usually given as the average GRPs per week measured during a 4-week period) to arrive at gross rating points. The figure is valuable because it combines indications of reach and frequency in a single calculation. GRP totals have been adapted in media planning as quick measures of advertising impact.

Needed:

    A. Audience value of each vehicle, expressed as a percentage (that is, percent reach). All figures must be of the same category; you cannot mix households with adults, or men with total audience, and so on.

    B. The number of times that each vehicle is used within the specified time period (that is, frequency of advertising insertion).

Formula:

       Gross rating points = Audience value in percent × Schedule frequency

or

       GRP = Reach% × Frequency

Steps to work the formula:

1. Find the rating values of each vehicle. (If the data are "raw" numbers, convert to percentages.)
2. Multiply the rating values from each vehicle by the number of times the vehicle appears in the advertising schedule.
3. Add the multiplied GRP for each vehicle to gain a sum total GRP figure for the period.

Example:

Radio

Daypart	Rating × Spots per week		GRP
M-F 4:00 P.M.–6:00 P.M.	2.2	10	22
Sat. 10:00 A.M.–3:00 P.M.	1.5	4	6
			Total GRP/Week = 28

Magazine

Publication	Average Issue Adult Women Readers × No. of Insertions		GRP
D	15	6	90
E	19	4	76
F	24	12	288
			Yearly GRP = 454

Unduplicated Reach

Unduplicated reach represents, through statistics, the probabilities of exposing a percentage of the households or persons by advertising in a certain media vehicle. Reach is calculated over a set time period, usually four weeks. The figure provides an estimate of how many different prospects might be exposed to an advertising schedule.

Needed:

A. From research sources, determine the estimated unduplicated audience figure.
B. Determine the base audience population. (Because reach is a percentage, the net audience must be compared to the highest possible population figure, which is the universe or base figure.)

Formulas:
Single Vehicle Reach

$$\text{Unduplicated reach} = \frac{\text{Unduplicated audience impressions}}{\text{Base population}}$$

Multiple Vehicle Reach
(This multiple vehicle calculation is a rough estimate because it uses a standard figure in calculating the overlap audiences of two or more vehicles. If the actual unduplicated figures are known, they should be used instead of this formula. Note that all reach figures are expressed in percent.)

[(Vehicle A Reach) + (Vehicle B Reach)] − [(Vehicle A Reach) × (Vehicle B Reach)] = Combined Reach of Vehicles A and B

Example:
An advertiser is using three magazines in an advertising schedule. Magazine A has a reach of 21 percent of the target group. Magazine B has a target reach of 15 percent, and Magazine C reaches 11 percent. What is the combined audience of all three magazines?

$$(A)\ 0.21\ +\ (B)\ 0.15\ =\qquad 0.36$$
$$\text{minus } (A)\ 0.21\ \times\ (B)\ 0.15\ =\qquad -0.03$$
$$\text{Equals } 0.33\ (\text{or, } 33\%)$$

Then, to combine the AB combination with C

$$(AB)\ 0.33\ +\ (C)\ 0.11\ =\qquad 0.44$$
$$\text{Minus } (AB)\ 0.33\ \times\ (C)\ 0.11\ =\qquad -0.04$$
$$\text{Equals } 0.40\ (\text{or, } 40\%)\ \text{combined reach}$$

Average Frequency of Exposure

Average frequency of exposure provides the repetition of exposure to a vehicle or a schedule of several vehicles. It is the number of times that the average audience exposed will likely see or hear the vehicles within a specified time period, usually four weeks.

Frequency is necessary to assure that a satisfactory portion of the audience reached will have adequate repeat exposure to remember or to react to the advertising message.

Needed:

A. The gross impressions from using a vehicle. (The impressions can be in "raw" numbers or in GRPs.)

B. The net impressions of a vehicle or vehicles. This is the unduplicated audience during the identical time period. (Again, figures can be "raw" numbers or percentages.)

Single Vehicle Formula:

$$\text{Average frequency} = \frac{\text{Gross impressions}}{\text{Net impressions}}$$

or,

$$\text{Average frequency} = \frac{\text{GRPs}}{\text{Reach}}$$

Example:

A magazine has an average single-issue audience of 20 percent reach to the target group, but using four issues will reach 30 percent of the target group. If the advertiser uses four issues, what is the average frequency?

$$\text{GRP} = 20 \times 4 = \frac{80}{30} = 2.7 \text{ average frequency}$$

Multiple Vehicles (for combined frequency) Formula:

$$\frac{[(\text{Vehicle A Reach}) \times (\text{Vehicle A Frequency})] + [\text{Vehicle B Reach}) \times (\text{Vehicle B Frequency})]}{\text{Unduplicated reach of A and B}}$$

Example:

Using a certain advertiser's schedule, radio station WXXX will reach 15 percent of Anytown households with a 6.5 frequency. If station WYYY is added, with a 20 percent reach and a 7.0 average frequency, what will be the combined frequency?

$$\frac{(15 \times 6.5) + (20 \times 7.0)}{32^*} = \frac{97.5 + 140}{32} = \frac{237.5}{32} = 7.4 \text{ combined average frequency}$$

*The combined reach of 20 percent and 15 percent is 32 percent, using our unduplicated reach formula:
$[(0.20) + (0.15)] - [(0.20) \times (0.15)] = [0.35] - [0.03] = 0.32$

Glossary of Advertising Media Terms

Accumulative audience. See *cumulative audience.*

Across the board. A program that is broadcast at the same time period every day (see *strip*).

Adjacency. A program or a commercial announcement that is adjacent to another on the same station, either preceding or following the other.

Affiliate. A broadcast station that grants to a network an option of specific times for broadcasting network programming, in return for compensation.

Agate line. Newspaper advertising space one column wide by one-fourteenth of an inch deep; often referred to simply as *line*; somewhat obsolete because most newspapers now use *column inch* measurements of advertising space, especially for national advertising.

Agency commission. Usually fifteen percent, allowed to advertising agencies by media on the agencies' purchase of media space or time.

Agency of record. Advertising agency that coordinates an advertiser's promotion of several products handled by more than a single agency (see *blanket contract*).

Agency recognition. Acknowledgment by media owners that certain advertising agencies are good credit risks and/or fulfill certain requirements, thus qualifying for a commission.

Air check. Recording a broadcast to serve as an archival or file copy.

Allotment. The number and type of outdoor posters in a showing (see *showing*).

Alternate sponsorship. Two advertisers who sponsor a single program; one advertiser sponsors one week and the other sponsors the alternate weeks (see *crossplugs*).

Announcement. An advertising message that is broadcast between programs (see *station break, participation, ID, billboard*) or an advertisement within a syndicated program or feature film; any broadcast commercial, regardless of time length, within or between programs that presents an advertiser's message or a public service message.

American Research Bureau (ARB). One of several national firms engaged in radio and television research; the founder of Arbitron ratings.

Annual rebate. See *rebate.*

Arbitron. A national broadcast ratings service.

Area of Dominant Influence (ADI). Arbitron measurement area that comprises those counties in which stations of a single originating market account for a greater share of the viewing households than those from any other market; similar to Nielsen's Designated Market Area.

Audience. Persons who receive an advertisement; individuals who read a newspaper or magazine, listen to a radio broadcast, view a television broadcast, etc.

Audience accumulation. The total number of different persons or households who are exposed to a single media vehicle over a period of time (see *cumulative audience*).

Audience composition. Audience analysis expressed in demographic terms or other characteristics.

Audience duplication. Those persons or households who see an advertisement more than once in a single media vehicle or in a combination of vehicles.

Audience flow. The movement of a broadcast audience's attention from one station to another when the program changes, measured against the audience that stays tuned to the same station or network to view the new program (see *holdover audience*).

Audience profile. The minute-by-minute viewing pattern for a program; a description of the characteristics of the people who are exposed to a medium or vehicle (see *profile*).

Audience turnover. That part of a broadcast audience that changes over time (see *audience flow*).

Audimeter. A. C. Nielsen Company's automatic device attached to radio or television receiving sets that records usage and station information (see *people meter*).

Availability. A broadcast time period that is open for reservation by an advertiser, in response to an advertiser's or agency's initial inquiry (slang *avail*).

Average audience. The number of broadcast homes that are tuned in for an average minute of a broadcast.

Average exposure. The average (mean) number of times that each audience member has been exposed to an advertisement.

Average net paid circulation. Average (mean) number of copies that a publication distributes per issue.

Back to back. Two broadcast programs or commercials in succession.

Basic rate. See *open rate.*

BAR (Broadcast Advertisers Report). A commercial broadcast monitoring service that is available on a network and market-by-market basis.

Barter. An advertising medium that sells time or space in return for merchandise or other non-monetary returns; also, a television programming offer where a station is offered a syndicated program in exchange for commercial positions within the program.

Billboard. An outdoor poster; cast and production information that follows a broadcast program; a six-second radio commercial; a short commercial announcement, usually eight or ten seconds in length, at the start and close of a program, announcing the name of the sponsor.

Billing. The value of advertising that is handled by an advertising agency on behalf of its clients (often called *billings*); the process of issuing invoices for media space and time that have been purchased.

Blanket contract. A special rate or discount that is granted by an advertising medium to an advertiser who advertises several products or services through more than one agency.

Bleed. Printing to the edge of the page, with no margin or border.

Block. Consecutive broadcast time periods.

Booking. Scheduling a broadcast program or commercial.

Brand Development Index (BDI). A comparative measure of a brand's sales in one market, compared with other markets, used to decide the relative sales value of one market versus another (see *Category Development Index*).

Break. Time available for purchase between two broadcast programs or between segments of a single program.

Bulk discount. A discount offered by media for quantity buys (see *quantity discount*).

Bulk rate. See *bulk discount*.

Business card. A small print advertisement, announcing a business, that does not change over time; see *rate holder*.

Business paper. A publication that is intended for business or professional interests.

Buy. The process of negotiating, ordering, and confirming the selection of a media vehicle and unit; as a noun, the advertising that is purchased from a vehicle.

Buyer. See *media buyer* and *media planner*.

Buying service. A company primarily engaged in the purchase of media for advertising purposes; it supplants part of the advertising agency media function; also called *media buying specialist* or *time/space buying specialist/service*.

Buy sheet. The form used by a media buyer to keep track of the data on a media selection buy.

Call letters. The letters that identify a station; e.g., WBZ-TV.

Campaign. A specific coordinated advertising effort on behalf of a particular product or service that extends for a specified period of time.

Car card. Transit advertisement in or on a bus, subway, or commuter train car.

Card rate. The cost of time or space listed on a rate card.

Carryover effect. The residual level of awareness or recall after a flight or campaign period; used to plan the timing of schedules.

Cash discount. A discount, usually two percent, by media to advertisers who pay promptly.

Category Development Index (CDI). A comparative market-by-market measure of a market's total sales of all brands of a single product category, used to evaluate the sales potential of a market for a product category or a brand (see *Brand Development Index*).

CC. The conclusion of a broadcast; e.g., this program runs 11:30 p.m.—CC.

Center spread. An advertisement appearing on two facing pages printed on a single sheet in the center of a publication (see *double truck*).

Chain. A broadcast network; also, a newspaper or magazine group of single ownership or control.

Chain break (CB). The time during which a network allows a station to identify itself; usually a twenty-second spot (slang *twenty*); now often a thirty-second spot plus a ten-second spot, with twenty seconds remaining for identification.

Checking. The process of confirming whether an advertisement actually appeared.

Checking copy. A copy of a publication that is supplied by the medium to show that an advertisement appeared as specified.

Circulation. In print, the number of copies distributed; in broadcast, the number of households within a signal area that have receiving sets; in outdoor, the number of people who have a reasonable opportunity to see a billboard.

City zone. A central city and the contiguous areas that cannot be distinguished from it.

City zone circulation. The number of newspapers that are distributed within a city, rather than in outlying areas.

Day-parts. Specific segments of the broadcast day; e.g., daytime, early fringe, prime time, late fringe, late night.

Deadline. The final date for accepting advertising material to meet a publication or broadcast schedule (see *closing date*).

Dealer imprint. Inserting a local dealer's identification into a nationally prepared advertisement.

Dealer tie-in. A manufacturer's announcement that lists local dealers; not the same as *co-op*.

Delayed broadcast (DB). A local station broadcasting a network program at a time other than its regularly scheduled network time.

Delivery. The ability to reach or communicate with a certain audience or number of people by using a particular advertising schedule; the physical delivery of a publication.

Demographic characteristics. The population characteristics of a group or audience.

Designated Market Area (DMA). A term used by the A. C. Nielsen Company; an area based on those counties in which stations of the originating market account for a greater share of the viewing households than those from any other area (see *ADI*); e.g., Lake County, Illinois, belongs to the Chicago DMA because a majority of household viewing in Lake County is or can be ascribed to Chicago stations rather than to stations from Milwaukee or any other market.

Digest unit. See *junior unit*.

Direct advertising. Advertising that is under complete control of the advertiser, rather than through some established medium; e.g., direct mail, free sampling, and so on.

Direct mail advertising. Advertising sent by mail; also used to describe advertising in other media that solicit orders directly through the mail.

Direct marketing. Sales made directly to the customer, rather than through middlemen or intervening channels; includes direct mail, direct advertising, telemarketing, and so on.

Directory advertising. Advertising that appears in a buying guide or directory; advertisements in a store directory; for example, Yellow Pages advertising.

Display advertising. Print advertising that is intended to attract attention and communicate easily through the use of space, illustrations, layout, headline, and so on, as opposed to classified advertising.

Display classified advertising. See *classified display advertising*.

Double spotting. See *piggyback*.

Double spread. See *two-page spread*.

Double truck. Slang term for a print advertisement that uses two full pages side-by-side, but not necessarily the two center pages, usually for a magazine advertisement (see *center spread* and *two-page spread*).

Drive time. Radio broadcast time during morning and evening commuter rush hours.

Earned rate. The advertising rate that is actually paid by the advertiser, after discounts and other calculations.

Effective frequency. Level or range of audience exposure that provides what an advertiser considers to be the minimal effective level, and no more than this optimal level or range; also called *effective reach*.

Effective reach. See *effective frequency*.

Facing. A billboard location with the panels facing the same direction and visible to the same lines of traffic.

Fixed rate. An advertising rate for advertising time that cannot be taken away or *preempted* by another advertiser; usually the highest advertising rate; commonly used in broadcast advertising.

Flat rate. A print advertising rate that is not subject to a discount.

Flight (flight saturation). Concentrating advertising within a short time period; an advertising campaign that runs for a specified number of weeks, followed by a period of inactivity (see *hiatus*), after which the campaign may resume with another flight.

Floating time. See *run of schedule*.

Forced combination. A policy to require newspaper advertisers to buy advertising space in both morning and evening newspapers owned by the same interests within a market.

Forcing distribution. Using advertising to increase consumer demand, thereby inducing dealers to stock a product; now seldom used.

Fractional page. Print advertising space of less than a full page.

Free circulation. A publication sent without charge; often with controlled circulation

Free-standing insert (FSI). Advertisement in a magazine or other publication that is not on a regular page; bound into the publication as a separate item.

Frequency. The number of times that an average audience member sees or hears an advertisement; the number of times that an individual or household is exposed to an advertisement or campaign (frequency of exposure); the number of times that an advertisement is run (frequency of insertion).

Frequency discount. A reduced advertising rate that is offered by media to advertisers who run a certain number of advertisements within a given time.

Fringe time. Broadcast time periods preceding or following prime time; television time between daytime and prime time is called *early fringe*, and the television time immediately following prime time is called *late fringe*.

Full run. One transit advertising car card in every transit bus or car.

General magazine. A consumer magazine that is not aimed at a special-interest audience.

Giveaway. A free offer; a broadcast program that offers free gifts as prizes.

Grid card. Spot broadcast advertising rates that are set in matrix format to allow a station to set rates based on current audience ratings and advertiser buying demand; for example,

	60-sec.	30/20-sec.	10-sec
A	$250	$175	$125
B	245	172	123
C	240	170	121
D	230	165	120

Gross Audience. The total number of households or people who are "delivered" or reached by an advertising schedule, without regard to any possible duplication that may occur; also called *total audience*.

Gross billing. The cost of advertising at the highest advertising rate; the total value of an advertising agency's space and time dealings (see *billing*).

Gross impressions. The total number of persons or the total number of audience impressions delivered by an advertising schedule; see *gross audience*.

Gross rate. The highest possible rate for advertising time or space.

Gross rating points (GRP). The total number of broadcast rating points delivered by an advertiser's television schedule, usually in a one-week period; an indicator of the combined audience percentage reach and exposure frequency achieved by an advertising schedule; in outdoor, a standard audience level upon which a market's advertising rates are based.

Gutter. The inside page margins where a publication is bound.

Half run. Transit advertising car cards in half the buses or transit cars of a system.

Head of household. The person within a family or household who is responsible for the major purchase decisions; sometimes, a male head and female head of household are considered separately.

Hiatus. A period during a campaign when an advertiser's schedule is suspended for a time, after which it resumes.

Hitchhiker. A broadcast advertising announcement at the end of a program that promotes another product from the same advertiser.

Holdover audience. Those persons tuned to a program who stay tuned to that station or network for the following program.

Horizontal cume. The total number of different people who were tuned to a broadcast station or network at the same time on different days of the week.

Horizontal publication. A business or trade publication that is of interest at one level or to one job function in a variety of businesses or fields.

House agency. An advertising agency that is owned or controlled by an advertiser.

House organ. A company's own publication.

H.U.R. Households using radio; see *sets in use*.

H.U.T. Households using television; see *sets in use* and *P.U.T.*

ID (Identification). A spot television commercial eight to ten seconds in length, during a station break; the last two seconds of the visual time may be reserved for showing the station call letters (*station identification*); a ten-second broadcast commercial announcement, sometimes referred to as a *ten*.

Impact. The degree to which an advertisement or campaign affects its audience; the amount of space (full-page, half-page, etc.) or of time (60-second, 30-second, etc.) that is purchased, as opposed to reach and frequency measures; also, the use of color, large type, powerful messages, or other devices that may induce audience reaction; see *unit*.

Independent station. A broadcast station that is not affiliated with a network.

Index. A numerical value that is assigned to quantitative data for ease of comparison.

Individual location. An outdoor location that has room only for one billboard.

Insert. An advertisement that is enclosed with bills or letters; a print advertisement, one-page or multi-page, that is distributed with the publication and may or may not be bound into it.

Insertion order. A statement from an advertising agency to a media vehicle that accompanies the advertisement copy and indicates specifications for the advertisement.

Integrated commercial. A broadcast advertising message that is delivered as part of the entertainment portion of a program.

Interactive media. Communications channels that provide for two-way interacting, such as CD-ROM multimedia systems or computer internet telecommunications.

Island position. A print advertisement that is surrounded by editorial material; a print advertisement that is not adjacent to any other advertising; a broadcast commercial that is scheduled away from any other commercial, with program content before and after; often at premium advertising rates.

Isolated 30. A thirty-second broadcast commercial that runs by itself and not in combination with any other announcement; usually found only on network television.

Junior unit. Permitting an advertiser to use a print advertisement that has been prepared for a smaller page size to be run in a publication with a larger page size, with editorial matter around it in the extra space; similarly, using a *Reader's Digest*-size advertising page in a larger magazine is usually called a *Digest unit*.

Key. A code in an advertisement to facilitate tracing which advertisement produced an inquiry or order.

Life. The length of time during which an advertisement is used; the length of time during which an advertisement is judged still to be effective; the length of time that a publication is retained by its audience.

Lifestyle profiles. Classifying media audiences on the basis of career, recreation, and/or leisure patterns or motives.

Linage. In print, the number of agate lines to be used for an advertisement or for a series of advertisements, now made somewhat obsolete by the declining use of agate-line measurements (see *agate line*).

Line rate. The print advertising rate that is established by the number of agate lines of space used; somewhat obsolete because of the declining use of agate line space measurements.

List broker. An agent who prepares and rents the use of mailing lists.

Local rate. An advertising rate offered by media to local advertisers that is lower than the rate offered to national advertisers.

Log. A broadcast station's record of its programming.

LOH (Ladies of the House). A term used by A. C. Nielsen Company in some of its reports, referring to female heads of households.

M. 1,000.

Magazine concept. Buying a certain number of broadcast announcements from a station with a certain guaranteed audience level, without selecting the specific times or programs.

Mail-order advertising. Advertisements intended to induce direct ordering of merchandise through the mail; the advertisements themselves are not necessarily distributed through the mail, and may appear in other advertising media.

Make-good. A repeat of an advertisement to compensate for an error, omission, or technical difficulty with the publication, broadcast, or transmission of the original.

Market. See *target market* and *target group*.

Market potential. The reasonable maximum market share or sales level that a product or service can be expected to achieve.

Market profile. A geographic description of the location of prospects for a product or service; sometimes used instead of *target profile*; see *target market* and *target profile*.

Market share. A company's or brand's portion of the sales of a product or service category.

Mat service. A service to newspapers that supplies pictures and drawings for use in advertisements; entire prepared advertisements may be offered; *mat* is slang for *matrix*.

Maximil rate. The cost of an agate line of advertising space at the highest milline rate; somewhat obsolete as the usage of agate lines has declined.

Media buyer. The person who is responsible for purchasing advertising space or time; often skilled in negotiation with the media.

Media planner. The person who is responsible for determining the proper use of advertising media to fulfill the marketing and promotional objectives for a specific product or advertiser.

Merchandising. The promotion of an advertiser's products, services, and the like to the sales force, wholesalers, and dealers; promotion other than advertising to consumers through the use of in-store displays, guarantees, services, point-of-purchase materials, and so on; display and promotion of retail goods; display of a mass media advertisement close to the point of sale.

Message distribution. Measurement of media audience by the successive frequency of exposure; for example, saw once, saw twice, and so on.

Metropolitan area. A geographic area consisting of a central city of 50,000 population or more, plus the economically and socially integrated surrounding area, as established by the federal government; usually limited by county boundaries; slang *metro area*.

Metro rating. The broadcast rating figure from within a metropolitan area.

Milline rate. A comparison of the advertising line rates of newspapers with uneven circulations by calculating the line rate per million circulation; determined by multiplying the line rate by 1,000,000 and dividing by the circulation; now somewhat obsolete because of the declining use of agate line measurements and advertising line rates.

Minimil rate. The cost of an agate line of advertising at the lowest possible milline rate; somewhat obsolete as the usage of agate lines has declined.

Mood programming. Maintaining a single approach or characteristic in broadcast programming.

NCR (or NCIR). Abbreviation for "no change in rate," used when some other format or specification change has occurred.

Net. Money paid to a media vehicle by an advertising agency after deducting the agency's commission; slang for *network*.

Net unduplicated audience. The number of different people who are reached by a single issue of two or more publications (see *cumulative audience*).

Network. In broadcast, a grouping of stations; an organization that supplies programming to a group or chain of stations.

Network cooperative program. A network program with provisions for inserting local commercials; see *cooperative program*.

Network option time. Broadcast time on a station for which the network has the option of selling advertising.

Newspaper syndicate. A firm that sells special material such as features, photographs, comic strips, cartoons, and so on, for publication in newspapers.

Next to reading matter. A print advertising position adjacent to news or editorial material; may be at premium rates.

Nielsen. The A. C. Nielsen Company; a firm engaged in local and national television ratings and other marketing research.

NSI. Nielsen Station Index; a rating service for individual, television stations.

NTI. Nielsen Television Index; a national television rating service, primarily for network programming.

O & O station. A broadcast station that is "owned and operated" by a network.

One-time rate. See *open rate*.

Open-end transcription. A transcribed broadcast with time for the insertion of local commercial announcements.

Open rate. The highest advertising rate before discounts can be earned; also called *basic rate* and *one-time rate*.

OTO. "One time only"; a commercial announcement that runs only once.

Overrun. Additional copies of an advertisement beyond the number actually ordered or needed; extra copies to replace damaged outdoor posters or transit car cards.

Package. A series of broadcast programs that an advertiser may sponsor.

Package plan discount. A spot television discount plan for buying a certain number of spots, usually within a one-week period.

Packager. An individual or company that produces packaged program series; also called *syndicator*.

Paid circulation. The number of print copies that are purchased by audience members.

Panel. A single outdoor billboard.

Participation. A commercial announcement within a broadcast program, as compared with one scheduled between programs; also called *participating announcements*.

Participation program. A broadcast program with each segment sponsored by a different advertiser.

Pass-along readers. Readers of a publication who acquire a copy other than by purchase or subscription; see *secondary audience*.

Pay cable. Cable television programming for which the audience must pay or subscribe.

Penetration. The percentage of households that have a broadcast receiving set; a measure of the degree of advertising effectiveness; the percentage of households that have been exposed to an advertising campaign.

People meter. Slang for a broadcast ratings measurement device that records individual audience members who are present during a program.

Per issue rate. A special magazine advertising rate that is determined by the number of issues that are used during the contract period; similar to a frequency discount, except not based on the number of advertisements, but rather on the number of issues in which an advertising campaign appears.

Piggyback. Slang for two of a sponsor's commercial announcements that are presented back-to-back within a single commercial time segment; for example, two 30-second commercials in a 60-second time slot; also called *double spotting*.

Pilot. A sample production of a proposed broadcast program series.

Plans board. An advertising agency committee that reviews campaign plans for clients.

Plug. A free mention of a product or service.

Point-of-purchase advertising (P.O.P.). Promotions in retail stores, usually displays.

Position. The location of an advertisement on a page; the time when a program or commercial announcement will run in a broadcast; special positions may cost premium prices.

Potential audience. The maximum possible audience.

Preemptible rate. An advertising rate that is subject to cancellation by another advertiser's paying a higher rate, usually in broadcast; the protection period varies by station, and ranges from no notice to two-weeks notice or more; see *fixed rate*.

Preemption. Cancellation of a broadcast program for special material or news; the right of a station or network to cancel a regular program to run a special program; a commercial announcement that may be replaced if another advertiser pays a higher or *fixed* rate.

Premium. An item that is offered to help promote a product or service; a higher-cost advertising rate (see *premium price*).

Premium price. A special advertising rate, usually higher, for special positions or other considerations.

Preprint. Advertising material that is printed in advance of the regular press run, perhaps on another printing press with greater capability for color, and so on.

Primary audience. Individuals in the print media audience who purchase or subscribe to the publication; see *secondary audience*.

Primary household. A household in which a publication has been subscribed to or purchased.

Primary listening area. The geographic area in which a broadcast transmission is static-free and easily received.

Primary readers. Those persons who purchase or subscribe to a publication; readers in primary households.

Prime time. The hours when viewing is at its peak on television; usually the evening hours.

Product allocation. The various products that are assigned to specific times or locations in an advertiser's schedule, where more than one brand is advertised; the amount of the advertising budget that is allocated to individual products.

Product protection. A time separation between the airing of broadcast commercial announcements for competitive goods or services.

Profile. A term used interchangeably with *audience composition* to describe the demographic characteristics of audiences.

Program compatibility. Broadcast programming or editorial content that is suitable for the product or service that is being promoted; suitability of the advertisement or campaign theme with program content.

Progressive proofs. A test press run of each color in the printing process.

Projected audience. The number of audience members calculated from a sample survey of audience size; the number of broadcast viewers, either in total or per receiving set, based on the sample for the rating percentages.

Publisher's statement. The certified circulation of a publication, attested by the publisher and subject to audit.

Pulp magazine. A publication, usually printed on low-quality paper, with sensational editorial material; for example, a mystery, detective, or ''TV/movie'' magazine.

Qualified circulation. The distribution of a publication that is restricted to individuals who meet certain requirements; for example, member physicians are qualified to receive *The Journal of the American Medical Association*.

Qualified reader. A person who can prove readership of a publication.

Quantity discount. A lower advertising rate for buying a certain amount of space or time.

Quarter-run. One-fourth of the car cards that are required for a full run in transit; a card in every fourth transit system vehicle.

Quintile. One-fifth of a group; usage in advertising often refers to audience members who have been divided into five equal groups (quintiles), ranging from the heaviest to the lightest media usage levels.

Rate. A charge for advertising media space or time.

Rate book. A printed book that is designed to provide advertising rates for several media vehicles; for example, Standard Rate and Data Service.

Rate card. A printed listing of advertising rates for a single media vehicle.

Rate differential. The difference between the local and the national advertising rates in a vehicle.

Rate guarantee. Media commitment that an advertising rate will not be increased during a certain calendar period.

Rate holder. A small print advertisement used by an advertiser to meet contract requirements for earning a discounted advertising rate.

Rate protection. The length of time that an advertiser is guaranteed a certain advertising rate without an increase.

Rating. The percentage of the potential broadcast audience that is tuned to a particular station, network, or program; the audience of a vehicle expressed as a percentage of the total population of an area.

Rating point. A rating of one percent; one percent of the potential audience; the sum of the ratings of multiple advertising insertions (for example, two advertisements with a rating of 10% each will total 20 rating points).

Reach. The total audience that a medium actually reaches; the size of the audience with which a vehicle communicates; the total number of people in an advertising media audience; the total percentage of the target group that is actually covered by an advertising campaign.

Reader interest. An expression of interest through inquiries, coupons, and so forth; the level of interest in various products.

Readership. The percentage or number of persons who read a publication or advertisement.

Reading notice. A print advertisement that is intended to resemble editorial matter.

Rebate. A payment that is returned by the media vehicle back to an advertiser who has overpaid, usually because of earning a lower rate than that originally contracted.

Reminder advertising. An advertisement, usually brief, that is intended to keep the name of a product or service before the public; often, a supplement to other advertising.

Rep. A media representative; slang term for a national sales representative.

Replacement. A substitute for a broadcast commercial announcement that did not clear the original order (that is, that was not broadcast as specified on the advertiser's order).

Retail trading zone (RTZ). The geographic area in which most of a market's population makes the majority of their retail purchases.

Roadblock or roadblocking. Slang term for placing television announcements at the same time on two or more networks or at the same time on several stations in a single market; used as a remedy to channel switching during a commercial break.

ROP color. Run-of-press color: color printing that is done during the regular press run.

Run of paper (ROP). Advertising that is positioned anywhere in a publication, with no choice of a specific place for the advertisement to appear.

Run of schedule (ROS). Broadcast commercial announcements that can be scheduled at the station's discretion anytime; in some cases, the advertiser can specify or request certain time periods; for example, ROS 10 a.m.–4 p.m. Monday-Friday.

Satellite station. A broadcast station in a fringe reception area, to boost the effective range of the main station's signal.

Saturation. An advertising media schedule of wide reach and high frequency, concentrated during a time period to achieve maximum coverage and impact (see *flight*).

Scatter plan. Commercial announcements that are scheduled during a variety of times in broadcast media; usually, the advertiser is permitted to specify general time periods during which the commercials will be scheduled; also called *scatter package*.

Schedule. A list of advertisements or media to be used in a campaign; a chart of the advertisements that have been planned.

Schedule and estimate. A data form submitted by an advertising agency to the advertiser prior to a firm media purchase; it contains price and audience goals and a proposed schedule.

Secondary audience. The members of a print media audience who do not subscribe to or purchase the publication; see *pass-along readers*.

Secondary listening area. The outlying area in which broadcast transmissions are subject to fading or static; in television, the Grade 3 signal contour.

Self-liquidating point-of-purchase. A display for which the retailer pays part or all of the costs.

Self-liquidating premium. An item for which the cost is paid by the customer; the price that the consumer pays covers the manufacturing cost of the premium.

Self-mailer. A direct-mail item that is mailed without an envelope.

Sets in use. The percentage of households that have broadcast receiving sets that are operating at one time within a market area; because many households have more than one receiving set, "households using television" and "households using radio" are the current common terms.

Share of audience ("share"). The percentage of sets-in-use (and thus of HUT or of HUR) that are tuned to a particular station, network, or program.

Shopping newspaper ("shopper"). A newspaper-like publication that is devoted to advertising, often distributed free to shoppers or to households.

Short rate. Money that is owed to a media vehicle by an advertiser to offset the rate differential between the earned rate and the lower contracted rate.

Showing. The number of outdoor posters that are necessary to reach a certain percentage of the mobile population in a market within a specified time; most outdoor markets are not purchased by Gross Rating Points; see *gross rating points*.

Sixty. Slang for a one-minute broadcast commercial announcement.

SNR. Abbreviation for "subject to nonrenewal"; commercial time that is available for purchase if the current advertiser does not renew.

Soap opera. Slang for a continuing broadcast dramatic serial, usually a daytime program.

Space buyer. The person who is responsible for purchasing advertising in newspapers, magazines, and business publications, and sometimes outdoor and transit; see *media buyer*.

Space position value. A measure of the effectiveness of an outdoor poster location.

Spectacular. A large outdoor lighted sign.

Split run. Testing two or more print advertisements by running each only to a portion of the audience, usually in a single issue.

Sponsor. An advertiser who buys the exclusive right to the time available for commercial announcements in a given broadcast program or segment.

Spot. The purchase of broadcast slots by geographic or station breakdowns; the purchase of slots at certain times, usually during station breaks; the term "'spot'" can refer to the time used for the commercial announcement or it can refer to the announcement itself.

Standard Metropolitan Statistical Area (S.M.S.A.). See *metropolitan area*.

Station break. The time between broadcast programs to permit station identification and spot announcements; slang for a 20-second broadcast announcement.

Station clearance. See *clear time*.

Station identification. The announcement of station call letters, usually with broadcast frequency or channel, and station location.

Station option time. A broadcast time for which the station has the option of selling advertising.

Station posters. Advertisements consisting of posters in transit stations.

Strip programming. A broadcast program or commercial that is scheduled at the same time of day on successive days of the week, either Monday through Friday or Monday through Sunday; see *across the board*.

Sunday supplement. A newspaper section in magazine format; also called *magazine supplement* or *magazine section* or simply *supplement*.

Sustaining period. A period of time during an advertising campaign when advertisements are used to remind the audience of the product or service or of the campaign; often, a time of reduced advertising expenditures following the introductory flight.

Sweep. The period of the year when a ratings service measures the broadcast audience in the majority of the markets throughout the country; for example, surveys that are scheduled for November 2 through 24 would be referred to as the "November sweep."

Syndicated program. Broadcast program that is sold to individual stations, rather than appearing on a network.

Syndicator. Television program distributor who works with reruns or new programs on a market-to-market basis; see *packager*.

Tabloid. A newspaper of the approximate size of a standard newspaper folded in half; slang *tab*.

Tag. Dealer identification, usually added to the end of a broadcast commercial announcement to indicate where the product or service being advertised can be purchased in the local market.

TBA. Abbreviation for "to be announced"; used as a notification in broadcast program schedules.

Target group. Those persons to whom a campaign is directed; those individuals with similar characteristics who are prospects for a product or service; also called *consumer profile*.

Target market. The geographic area or areas to which a campaign is directed; the areas where a product is being sold or introduced; also called *market profile*.

Target profile. A demographic description of the target groups, often including the geographic target markets.

Tearsheet. A publication page with an advertiser's message, sent to the advertiser for approval or for checking.

Teaser. An advertisement that precedes the major portion of an advertising campaign, intended to build curiosity.

Telemarketing. Selling by use of telephones, either initiating the calls or receiving orders.

Ten. Slang for a 10-second broadcast commercial announcement.

TF. A newspaper insertion order abbreviation for "till forbidden"; run the advertisement until told to stop.

Thirty. Slang for a 30-second broadcast commercial announcement.

Throwaways. Free shopping newspapers.

Tie-in. See *cooperative advertising* and *dealer tie-in*.

Time buyer. The person who is responsible for purchasing advertising on radio and television; see *media buyer*.

Time sheet. A form used by a time buyer to keep track of the data on a media buy; also called a *buy sheet*; also, the form used to keep track of how advertising agency personnel use their time, for application in billing purposes.

Total audience. The number of all the different homes or individuals who are tuned to a broadcast program for six minutes or longer.

TPR. Abbreviation for "time period rating"; the rating for a particular broadcast time period, regardless of the program that was broadcast during that slot.

Trade paper. A specialized publication for a specific profession, trade, or industry; another term for some business publications.

Traffic count. The number of persons who pass an outdoor panel location.

Trim size. The final magazine page size, after it is trimmed.

Turnover. The frequency with which the audience for a broadcast program changes over a period of time; see *audience turnover*.

Twenty. Slang for a 20-second broadcast commercial announcement; also called a *chain break* or *station break*.

Two-page spread. A single print advertisement that crosses two facing pages; also called *double spread* or *double truck*; see *center spread* and *double truck*.

Unduplicated audience. The total number of different people who were exposed to an advertisement or campaign through multiple insertions in more than one media vehicle; see *cumulative audience*.

Unit (advertising unit). The form and context in which an advertisement appears in a media vehicle; for example, full-page, half-page vertical, center spread, black-and-white, back cover, two-color; 30-second commercial, 10-second ID, and so on.

Upfront buying, Initial purchasing of network television advertising by firms wishing to have optimal selection of available programs; reserving advertising time on network television programs when the seasonal schedule is first announced; this tactic often requires longer schedules and higher prices.

Usage level. Classifying media audiences by the amount of the product or service they use.

Vehicle. An individual outlet of an advertising medium, such as a certain magazine or a specific broadcast station or program.

Vertical cume. The total number of different people who were tuned to successive broadcast programs.

Vertical publication. A business or trade publication that is of interest to all levels or job functions within a single business or profession.

Vertical saturation. Many broadcast commercial announcements scheduled throughout the course of a single day, generally designed to reach many different people, in an attempt to reach a high percentage of the broadcast audience.

Wait order. An instruction or request to delay publication of a print advertisement; also but seldom used in broadcast.

Waste circulation. The readers of a publication who are not prospects for the product or service being advertised; advertisement distribution in an area in which the product or service is not distributed.

Index

Class magazines. Special-interest magazines with desirable up-scale audiences.

Classified advertising. Advertising that is set in small type and arranged according to categories or interests.

Classified display advertising. Classified advertising of a larger size than most other classified advertising, possibly with head-lines, illustrations, etc.; classified advertising with some of the characteristics of display advertising (see *display advertising*).

Clearance. Coverage of national television households by the number of stations (or markets) accepting a network program for airing; also, gaining available time on stations to carry a program or commercial.

Clear time. The process of reserving time or time periods with a station or network; checking on available advertising time.

Clipping bureau. An organization that aids in checking print advertising, by clipping the advertisements from print media.

Closing date. The final deadline set by print media for adver-tising material to appear in a certain issue; in broadcast, the term *closing hour* may be used.

Closure. A sale resulting from following up on an inquiry from direct mail advertising.

Column inch. Publication space that is one column wide by one inch high, used as a measure of advertising space.

Combination rate. A special discounted advertising rate for buying space in two or more publications owned by the same interests.

Commercial impressions. The total audience, including dupli-cation, for all commercial announcements in an advertiser's schedule; see *gross impressions*.

Confirmation. A broadcast media statement that a specific time is still open for purchase by an advertiser who is prepar-ing a broadcast advertising schedule.

Consumer profile. A demographic description of the people or households that are prospects for a product or service; see *tar-get group*.

Contiguity rate. A reduced broadcast advertising rate for spon-soring two or more programs in succession; e.g., an advertiser participating in two programs running from 7:00–7:30 and then 7:30–8:00 may qualify for a contiguity rate.

Controlled circulation. Circulation that is limited to persons who qualify to receive a publication; often distributed free to qualified persons.

Cooperative advertising. Retail advertising that is paid partly or fully by a manufacturer; two or more manufacturers cooper-ating in a single advertisement; slang *co-op*.

Cooperative announcement. Commercial time that is made available in network programs to stations for sale to local or na-tional advertisers.

Cooperative program. A network broadcast that is also sold on a local basis and sponsored by both national and local advertisers; e.g., "The Tonight Show"; see *network coopera-tive program*.

Corporate discounting. Incentives offered to advertisers with numerous brands of products; all of the corporation's advertis-ing schedules are combined for a larger discount level.

Cost per thousand (CPM). A dollar comparison that shows the relative cost of various media or vehicles; the figure indicates the dollar cost of advertising exposure to a thousand house-holds or individuals.

CPM/PCM. Cost per thousand per commercial minute; the cost per thousand households or individuals of a minute of broadcast advertising time.

CPR. Cost per rating point (see *rating point*); the figure indi-cates the dollar cost of advertising exposure to one percentage point of the target group, audience, or population.

Cover position. An advertisement on the cover of a publica-tion, often at a premium cost; the *first cover* is the outside front cover; the *second cover* is the inside front cover; the *third cover* is the inside back cover; the *fourth cover* is the outside back cover.

Coverage. The number or percentage of individuals or house-holds that are exposed to a medium or to an advertising campaign.

Cowcatcher. A brief commercial announcement at the begin-ning of a broadcast program.

Crossplugs. In alternating sponsorships, permitting each adver-tiser to insert one announcement into the program during the weeks when the other advertiser is the sponsor, maintaining weekly exposure for both (see *alternate sponsorship*).

Cumulative audience (cume). Cumulative broadcast rating; the net unduplicated audience of a station or network during two or more time periods; also used to describe how many dif-ferent households or people are reached by an advertising schedule (also called *accumulative audience, net audience,* and *unduplicated audience*); technically, a cumulative audience is those persons who were exposed to any insertion of an adver-tisement in multiple editions of a single vehicle, whereas undu-plicated audience is those persons who were exposed to any in-sertion of an advertisement in a combination of vehicles or media, counting each person only once.

Cumulative reach. The number of different households that are exposed to a medium or campaign during a specific time.

Cut-in. The insertion of a local commercial announcement into a network or recorded program.